EASY Javascript - Handy Guide

Discover the World of Web Programming

INDEX

Intro

Welcome to "EASY JavaScript - Handy Guide". If you are looking for an easy and accessible way to learn JavaScript, you have made the right choice.

In recent years, web programming has become increasingly relevant, with JavaScript emerging as one of the most widely used and powerful programming languages for developing interactive web applications. With JavaScript, you can create dynamic Web sites, add interactivity to page elements, handle asynchronous calls to servers, and even create engaging games.

This guide is designed for those who want to enter the world of web programming with a practical and effective approach. Whether you are a complete beginner or already have some basic knowledge of HTML and CSS, this manual has been structured to walk you step by step through the process of learning JavaScript.

With this guide, you will be able to gain a solid understanding of the fundamentals of JavaScript and develop the skills you need to create interactive Web applications. We will start with basic concepts such as variables, operators, and control structures, and then delve into topics such as functions, arrays, objects, and DOM manipulation. We will also learn how to handle errors, work with APIs for sending and receiving data, and implement asynchronous programming.

Our goal is to make learning JavaScript an accessible and fun experience. The guide is full of practical examples that will help you put what you have learned into practice. In addition, you will find useful tips and tricks to optimize your code and improve the performance of your applications.

Get ready to discover the fascinating world of web programming with JavaScript. We are excited to accompany you on this journey to success and exploration of JavaScript's endless potential.

Enjoy learning and have fun!

Development Environment

Introduction

This guide includes a dedicated development environment, which means it avoids the need to set up a local development environment, which may vary from computer to computer. Using the included development environment is more convenient and faster, as no software installation is required. In addition, it will be possible to test written pages directly from the browser.

Configuration

To access the dedicated development environment, log on to https://easy-code.cloud/board . After registering or logging in, you will immediately find the work environment ready to use.

To create a new page click on the 'add' button in the left side column. Enter a name for the page respecting the constraints, choose the desired language via the drop-down menu and finally press 'Create'. You will find a summary of all the pages you have created in the left side column.

To write on a page click on its name: the text editor will open, allowing you to write code on it.

Follow these steps:

- Create an HTML file: it will serve as the entry point for your JavaScript application. You can call it index.html, for example. You can use the code editor to create and edit the HTML file.

- Link your JavaScript file to your HTML file: within your HTML file, add a <script> tag to link your JavaScript file. You can do this by using a <script src="filename.js"></script> tag, where "filename.js" represents the name of your JavaScript file.

- Create your JavaScript file: create a JavaScript file using your code editor. You can call it filename.js, for example.

- Write JavaScript code: within your JavaScript file, you can start writing JavaScript code for your application.

- Open the previous HTML page created using the appropriate button.

- To view the browser console, right-click on the page, then click 'Inspect' and finally look for the 'Console' tab.

Introduction to JavaScript

JavaScript history

JavaScript is an interpreted, object-oriented, event-driven programming language that has become fundamental to the development of interactive Web applications. Created by Brendan Eich in 1995, JavaScript began as a scripting language to enhance the interactivity of Web pages.

In the latter half of the 1990s, the World Wide Web was experiencing rapid growth, and static Web pages were becoming increasingly common. However, there was a clear need to introduce interactive elements into web pages to enhance the user experience. This was the context in which JavaScript was born.

Brendan Eich, who worked for Netscape Communications Corporation (now Mozilla Corporation), was commissioned to create a scripting language for the Netscape Navigator browser. The goal was to provide Web developers with a simple and powerful tool for adding interactivity to Web pages.

Within weeks, Eich created the first prototype of JavaScript, originally called "Mocha" and later renamed to "LiveScript." In September 1995, when Netscape Navigator 2.0 was released, the language was permanently renamed to JavaScript, probably to take advantage of the popularity of the Java language, although the similarities between the two languages are limited.

Meanwhile, Microsoft was developing Internet Explorer and decided to create its own scripting language for the browser. Microsoft called its language "JScript," but it was actually a compatible version of JavaScript to allow for greater interoperability between the two browsers.

JavaScript has continued to evolve over the years, with the introduction of new versions and specifications defined by Ecma International, the standards-setting organization for the language. The most significant version was JavaScript 1.5 in 1999.

Over the past few decades, JavaScript has become extremely popular and gained wide adoption in the world of web development. It has contributed to the emergence of many technologies and frameworks, such as jQuery, Angular, React and Node.js, which have expanded its capabilities and made its use even more widespread.

Today, JavaScript is used not only for website development, but also for the development of complex web applications, hybrid mobile applications, server-side scripting, and more. It has become one of the most important and indispensable programming languages for web developers.

JavaScript has certainly left a significant imprint on the history of computing, transforming the web browsing experience and paving the way for new opportunities and innovations in the world of web development.

Using JavaScript on the Web

JavaScript adds special functionality and behavior to web pages that would normally be static and without action. For example, when you visit a website and have the opportunity to fill out a form, such as a registration form or contact form, JavaScript is used to check whether you have entered all the required information correctly. If not, it may show you an error message or highlight fields that need attention.

It is also used to add visual effects and animations to web pages. For example, you might see elements that move or change color when you hover your mouse over them. These effects are created using JavaScript to change the way HTML elements are displayed and react to events.

JavaScript is also used to handle events that occur during a user's interaction with a web page. For example, when you click a button or scroll down a page, JavaScript can detect these events and react by performing specific actions, such as showing more information or loading new content without having to reload the entire page.

It also allows asynchronous calls to the server to get or send data without having to refresh the entire page. This allows for more fluid and responsive user experiences, such as when you post a comment in a social network or add a product to a shopping cart while shopping online.

In summary, JavaScript is a programming language that is used on the Web to make pages interactive, manipulate HTML elements, handle events, and add special features such as form validation, animations, and asynchronous calls. Without JavaScript, many of the interactive and dynamic features we see on the Web today would not be possible.

Features and benefits of the language

Below we list some of the main features of Javascript.

- **Ease of use**: JavaScript is a relatively simple programming language to learn. Its syntax is similar to that of English, and there are many resources available online to help you get started. You can write JavaScript code directly within HTML files, making the learning and development process much easier.

- **Wide adoption**: JavaScript is widely supported by all modern browsers, which means that the JavaScript code you write will work on many different devices. You don't need to worry about compatibility differences between browsers.

- **Interactivity**: JavaScript allows you to add interactivity to web pages. You can create buttons that react to clicks, drop-down menus that change content based on the user's selection, and forms that check if the data entered is correct. This makes web pages more engaging and efficient for users.

- **Manipulation of page elements**: JavaScript allows you to manipulate web page elements, such as text, images, and video. You can change their content, style and position on the page dynamically. This gives you complete control over the presentation of your content.

- **Data validation**: JavaScript can be used to check if the data entered into a form is correct. For example, you can check if an email address is in the correct format or if a field has been filled in before submitting a form. This helps ensure that the data entered by users is correct and consistent.

- **Support for asynchronous programming**: JavaScript supports asynchronous programming, which allows you to perform operations without blocking the execution of the rest of the code. For example, you can load content from a server or send requests to an API without interrupting the user experience. This makes your web applications more fluid and responsive.

- **Large developer community**: JavaScript has a large and active developer community that shares resources, libraries, and frameworks. You can find numerous tutorials, documentation, and online forums that will help you learn and solve any problems you encounter during development.

Basic concepts

Variables and data types

In JavaScript, variables are used to store and manipulate data. You can declare a variable using the var, let or const keyword, followed by the desired name of the variable.

There are several data types you can assign to variables in JavaScript. Here are some of the most common data types:

Numbers: Numbers represent numerical values. They can be integers (such as 1, 2, 3) or decimals (such as 3.14, 2.5). For example:

```
var age = 25;
var price = 9.99;
```

Strings: Strings represent a sequence of characters delimited by single (") or double ("") quotation marks. For example:

```
var name = "John";
var message = 'Hello, world!';
```

Booleans: Booleans represent a truth value, which can be true or false. For example:

```
var isLogged = true;
var hasPermission = false;
```

Array: An array is an ordered collection of elements, separated by commas and enclosed in square brackets ([]). The elements can be of any data type, including another array. For example:

```
var numbers = [1, 2, 3, 4, 5];
var names = ["John", "Jane", "Alice"];
```

Objects: Objects represent a collection of key-value pairs, enclosed in curly brackets ({}). Each key-value pair is separated by a comma. For example:

```
var person = {
  name: "John",
  age: 25,
  isStudent: true
};
```

Null and **undefined**: null represents the intentional absence of a value, while undefined indicates that a variable has not been initialized or does not have an assigned value.

```
var x = null;
var y;
```

These are just some of the basic data types in JavaScript. The language also supports more advanced data types, such as dates, symbols, and functions.

Remember that in JavaScript, variables are dynamic, which means that they can hold different types of data over time.
Unlike some other programming languages, you do not have to specify the data type when declaring a variable.

This means that a variable can be initially assigned to a value of a certain data type and later be reassigned to a value of a completely different data type. For example:

```
var x = 10; // x is a number
x = "Hello"; // x is now a string
x = true; // x is now a boolean
```

In this example, the variable x is initially assigned to the value 10, which is a number. Next, it is reassigned to the value "Hello," which is a string. Finally, it is reassigned to the value true, which is a boolean.

This flexibility of dynamic variables in JavaScript can be very useful in many scenarios. For example:

- You can use the same variable to keep track of data of different types in different parts of your program.
- You can change the data type of a variable depending on conditions or events that occur during program execution.
- You can perform data type conversion operations implicitly or explicitly.

However, it is important to be aware of this feature and make sure that variables are used consistently in your code. If a variable is initialized with a certain data type and then reassigned to a different data type, it could result in unexpected behavior or errors in your program.

Also, it is always good practice to assign meaningful names to variables that reflect their purpose and the type of data they are supposed to hold. This can make your code more readable and reduce the risk of type errors.

Comments, semicolon and capital letters

You can use comments to insert notes or explanations into the code without affecting the execution of the program. There are two types of comments in JavaScript:

Single-line comments: They are created using **//**. Anything that follows // on the same line is considered a comment and is not executed by the program. Example:

```
// This is a single line comment
```

```
var x = 5; // This comment explains the assignment of the variable x
```

Multi-line comments: They are created using **/*** to start the comment and ***/** to end it. Anything between /* and */ is considered a comment and is not executed. Example:

```
/*
This is a comment
on multiple lines
*/
var y = 10; // This comment explains the assignment of the variable y
```

Semicolons (;) are used in JavaScript to separate instructions. Although in some cases the semicolon can be omitted, it is a good practice to always include it at the end of each instruction to avoid possible misinterpretation by the JavaScript engine. Example:

```
var a = 5;
var b = 10;
var sum = a + b;
```

JavaScript is a **case sensitive** programming language, which means that it distinguishes between uppercase and lowercase letters. This means that when writing JavaScript code, attention must be paid to the correct use of upper and lower case letters.

For example, the following statements represent two distinct variables in JavaScript:

```
var myVariable = 10;
var myvariable = 20;
```

In this case, myVariable and myvariable are considered two different variables because of the difference in the initial letter.

Case sensitivity also applies to function names, identifiers, language keywords, and function calls. So be sure to always use the correct combination of uppercase and lowercase letters when referring to variables, functions, or keywords in JavaScript.

Here are some examples to illustrate case sensitivity in JavaScript:

```
var myVariable = 10;
console.log(myVariable); // Output: 10

console.log(myvariable); // Error: variable myvariable is not defined

function myFunction() {
  console.log("Hello!");
}
```

```
myFunction(); // Output: Hello!

MyFunction(); // Error: myFunction function is not defined
```

Regarding spaces, JavaScript is a "white space insensitive" language, which means that white spaces such as spaces, tabs, and carriage returns are ignored. However, the use of white spaces can improve the readability of code. It is advisable to use spaces to separate operators, terms, parentheses and function arguments to make the code clearer and more understandable.

Example:

```
var result = (a + b) * c;
var greeting = "Hello, " + name + "!";
```

Output

In JavaScript, output can be displayed in the browser or console using different instructions. Here are some of the most common options for output:

Console.log():
The console.log() statement is used to print values in the browser console or development environment. It can be used to display variables, strings, calculation results, and more. Example:

```
var message = "Hello, world!"
console.log(message); // Print "Hello, world!" in the console
```

Alert():
The alert() statement is used to display an alert window in the browser with the specified text. It is useful for displaying immediate messages to the user. Example:

```
var message = "Hello, world!"
alert(message); // Show an alert window with the message "Hello, world!"
```

Document.write():
The document.write() instruction is used to write content directly into the HTML document. It can be used to display text, variables, or dynamic HTML. Example:

```
var message = "Hello, world!"
document.write(message); // Writes "Hello, world!" in the HTML document
```

However, document.write() can overwrite the entire HTML document if it is called after the page initially loads, so it is often preferable to use other techniques for adding dynamic content.

InnerHTML:
The innerHTML attribute can be used to modify the content of a specific HTML element. It can be used to display text, variables or dynamic HTML within a specific element on the page. Example:

```
var message = "Hello, world!"
document.getElementById("myElement").innerHTML = message; // Edit the content of the element with id
"myElement"
```

In this example, getElementById() is used to get a reference to the HTML element with the id "myElement," and then its content is modified using innerHTML. We will address this latter mode of manipulating the content of HTML pages in more detail in later chapters.

Operators and expressions

In JavaScript, operators are used to perform operations on values or variables and combine different expressions to obtain desired results. Expressions, on the other hand, are combinations of values, variables, and operators that produce a value.

Here are some of the most common operators in JavaScript:

Arithmetic operators:
+ (addition): adds two values together.
- (subtraction): subtracts one value from another.
* (multiplication): multiplies two values.
/ (division): divides one value by another.
% (modulo): returns the remainder of an integer division.
++ (increment): increases a value by 1.
- - (decrement): decreases a value by 1.

Example:

```
var x = 5;
var y = 3;
var sum = x + y; // 8
var difference = x - y; // 2
var product = x * y; // 15
var quotient = x / y; // 1.6666666666666666666666666666667
var remainder = x % y; // 2
x++; // x divides 6
y--; // y divides 2
```

Assignment operators:
= (assignment): assigns a value to a variable.
+=, -=, *=, /=, %=: combine the assignment operation with an arithmetic operation.

Example:

```
var x = 10;
x += 5; // Equivalent to x = x + 5; => x divides 15
```

Comparing operators:

   == (equality): checks whether two values are equal.
   != (different): checks whether two values are different.
   > (greater): checks whether one value is greater than another.
   < (less): checks whether one value is less than another.
   >= (greater or equal): checks whether one value is greater than or equal to another.
   <= (less than or equal): checks whether one value is less than or equal to another.

Example:

```
var a = 5;
var b = 3;
var isEqual = (a == b); // false
var isNotEqual = (a != b); // true
var isGreater = (a > b); // true
var isLess = (a < b); // false
var isGreaterOrEqual = (a >= b); // true
var isLessOrEqual = (a <= b); // false
```

Logical operators:

   && (logical AND): returns true if both conditions are true.
   || (logical OR): returns true if at least one of the conditions is true.
   ! (NOT logical): negates a condition, returning the opposite value.

Example:

```
var x = 5;
var y = 10;
var isTrue = (x < 10 && y > 5);  // true
var isFalse = (x > 10 || y < 5);  // false
var isNotTrue = !(x < 10);  // false
```

There are also other operators such as bitwise operators, string concatenation operators, and array element and object access operators.

Expressions, then, combine values and operators to generate a value. For example:

```
var result = (x + y) * 2;
```

In this example, the expression (x + y) sums the values of x and y, then the result is multiplied by 2 to obtain the final value assigned to result.

These are just the basic concepts of operators and expressions in JavaScript. There are many other nuances and advanced operators that can be used in more complex situations, but these should give you a good foundation to start with.

Data type conversion

Data type conversion is the process of transforming one data type into another. This conversion can be implicit, when JavaScript automatically performs the conversion, or explicit, when the programmer explicitly specifies the conversion.

Here are some examples of data type conversion in JavaScript:

Implicit conversion:

```
var x = 5; // x is of type number
var y = "10"; // y is of type string
var sum = x + y; // JavaScript implicitly converts x to a string and concatenates the values: "510"
```

In this example, during the concatenation operation, JavaScript implicitly converts the numeric value x to a string to obtain the desired result.

Explicit conversion:

- String-to-number conversion:

```
var x = "5"; // x is of type string
var y = parseInt(x); // y is of type number, converted from x using the parseInt() function
```

In this example, the parseInt() function explicitly converts the string "5" to a numeric value 5.

- Number-to-string conversion:

```
var x = 5; // x is of type number
var y = x.toString(); // y is of type string, converted from x using the toString() method
```

Here, the toString() method is used to explicitly convert the number x to a string.

- String-to-boolean conversion:

```
var x = "true"; // x is of type string
var y = Boolean(x); // y is of type Boolean, converted from x using the Boolean() function
```

In this case, the Boolean() function is used to convert the string "true" to a Boolean true value.

There are also other functions and methods for converting data types, such as parseFloat(), Number(), String(), etc.

It is important to keep in mind that when converting data types, information loss or unexpected behavior can occur, so care must be taken when working with complex data type conversions.

Control structures

Control structures in JavaScript are used to manage the flow of code execution, allowing decisions to be made and iterating over a set of instructions based on certain conditions. The main control structures include the conditional if and else statements, the switch statement and loops such as for, while and do...while. We will explore each of these control structures in detail:

Conditional if and else statement:
The if statement allows you to execute a block of code if a certain condition is true. If the condition is false, the if statement can be used to execute a different block of code. Example:

```
var x = 5;
if (x > 0) {
  console.log("x is positive");
} else {
  console.log("x is negative or zero");
}
```

In this example, if x is greater than zero, the message "x is positive" will be displayed. Otherwise, the message "x is negative or zero" will be displayed.

Switch statement:
The switch statement allows different actions to be performed based on different cases. An expression is provided that is evaluated and compared with the cases specified within the switch. If a match is found, the associated code block is executed. Example:

```
var day = "Monday";
switch (day) {
  case "Monday":
    console.log("Today is Monday");
    break;
  case "Tuesday":
    console.log("Today is Tuesday");
    break;
  default:
    console.log("Today is another day of the week");
}
```

In this example, if day is "Monday," the message "Today is Monday" will be displayed. If day is "Tuesday," the message "Today is Tuesday" will be displayed. If day does not match any of the specified cases, the default message will be displayed.

Loops:
Loops allow a block of code to be executed repeatedly until a certain condition is met. In JavaScript, there are mainly three types of loops: for, while and do...while.

For:
The for loop is used to execute a block of code a specified number of times. A start condition, a termination condition and an increment/decrement operation are provided. Example:

```
for (var i = 0; i < 5; i++) {
  console.log(i);
}
```

In this example, the for loop is executed five times, printing the numbers 0 to 4.

While:
The while loop is used to execute a block of code as long as a certain condition is true. Example:

```
var i = 0;
while (i < 5) {
  console.log(i);
  i++;
}
```

In this example, the while loop is executed as long as i is less than 5, printing the numbers 0 to 4.

Do...while:
The do...while loop is similar to the while loop, but is executed at least once, regardless of the validity of the condition. After each iteration, the condition is checked to decide whether to continue or exit the loop. Example:

```
var i = 0;
do {
  console.log(i);
  i++;
} while (i < 5);
```

In this case, the do...while loop is executed at least once, printing 0, and then executed until i is less than 5.

Control structures in JavaScript provide a flexible way to manage the flow of code execution based on conditions and to execute blocks of code repeatedly.

Break and continue

Break and continue instructions are used within loops to control the flow of execution.

Break:
The break instruction is used to stop the execution of a loop early, even if the termination condition has not been reached. Example with the for loop:

```
for (var i = 0; i < 5; i++) {
  if (i === 3) {
    break;
  }
  console.log(i);
}
```

In this example, when the value of i becomes 3, the break statement is executed and the for loop is interrupted, so the number 3 will not be printed. The output will be: 0, 1, 2.

Continue:
The continue instruction is used to skip the current iteration of a loop and move on to the next one. Example with the for loop:

```
for (var i = 0; i < 5; i++) {
  if (i === 2) {
    continue;
  }
  console.log(i);
}
```

In this example, when the value of i becomes 2, the continue instruction is executed, skipping the current iteration. So the number 2 will not be printed. The output will be: 0, 1, 3, 4.

Both break and continue statements can be used with different types of loops such as for, while and do...while. They allow more control over the flow of execution within loops, allowing specific actions to be performed based on certain conditions.

Functions

Defining and calling functions

Defining and calling functions is a fundamental aspect of programming in JavaScript.
Functions are reusable blocks of code that perform a specific action when called. Functions allow code to be organized into logical units and perform certain actions repetitively or when needed.

Defining a function:
To define a function, we use the keyword function, followed by the function name and a pair of round brackets (). We can also specify any parameters within the brackets, which represent the input values that the function can accept. Example of a function definition without parameters:

```
function greet() {
  console.log("Hello, world!");
}
```

In this example, we defined a function called greet() that accepts no parameters. When this function is called, it will print "Hello, world!" in the console.

Calling a function:
To call a function, we use the function name followed by a pair of round brackets (). If the function accepts parameters, we can pass the desired values inside the round brackets. Example of calling a function without parameters:

```
greet();
```

In this case, we are calling the greet() function without any parameters. The function will print "Hello, world!" in the console.

Parameters and arguments

In JavaScript, functions can accept parameters, which are variables used to receive input or data from the function call. When a function is called, the arguments are the specific values passed as input for the function's parameters. Below is a more detailed explanation of function parameters and arguments in JavaScript.

Defining the parameters of a function:
To define the parameters of a function, they are listed in brackets () in the function declaration. Parameters are variable names that will be used within the body of the function to represent input values. Example of a function definition with parameters:

```
function greet(name, age) {
  console.log("Hello, " + name + "! You are " + age + " years old.");
}
```

In this example, we defined a function called greet() that accepts two parameters: name and age. Within the body of the function, we can use these parameters to process and generate custom output.

Calling a function with arguments:
To call a function and pass specific values to its parameters, we place the arguments in round brackets ()
when calling the function. The arguments can be literals, variables, or expressions that generate the desired values. Example of calling a function with arguments:

```
greet("Mary", 25);
```

In this case, we are calling the greet() function with two arguments, "Mary" and 25. These values will be assigned to the function's name and age parameters, respectively. The output will be "Hello, Mary! You are 25."

We can also pass variables as function arguments:

```
var name = "Bob";
var age = 30;
greet(name, age);
```

In this example, we are declaring two variables name and age and then passing them as arguments to the greet() function. The output will be "Hello, Bob! You are 30 years old."

It is important to note that the number of arguments passed when calling a function should match the number and order of the parameters defined in the function. Otherwise, the values may be misinterpreted or an error may occur.

Function parameters in JavaScript are very flexible, allowing you to create functions that accept no parameters, a specific number of parameters, or even a variable number of parameters. This allows you to write functions that adapt to different situations and requirements in your code.

Return statement

Functions can also return values using the **return** statement. This allows a specific result to be obtained from the function that can be used or assigned to other variables.
The return statement stops the execution of the function and returns the specified value.

Here is an example of a function with the return statement:

```
function sum(a, b) {
  return a + b;
}
```

In this example, we defined a function called sum() that accepts two parameters a and b. The return statement is used to return the sum of a and b as the result of the function.

We can call this function and assign the returned value to a variable:

```
var result = sum(3, 4);
console.log(result); // Output: 7
```

In this case, the function sum(3, 4) returns the value 7, which is then assigned to the result variable. Next, the result value is printed in the console.

The return statement can be used to return any type of value, such as numbers, strings, objects, or even other functions.

It is important to note that the use of the return statement terminates the execution of the function. Therefore, any code following the return statement within the same function will not be executed.

```
function greet(name) {
  if (!name) {
    return; // Terminate function execution if name parameter is empty
  }
  return "Hello, " + name + "!"
}

console.log(greet("Mary")); // Output: "Hello, Mary!"
console.log(greet()); // Output: undefined (no value returned)
```

In the example above, if the name parameter is empty, the return statement is used to immediately terminate the execution of the function. If a name is provided, the function will return the corresponding greeting message. If no name is provided, the function will not return any value and thus the result will be undefined.

Using the return statement is useful for obtaining and using the return value of a function elsewhere in your code, allowing you to perform operations or decision making based on that value.

Scope of variables

The scope of variables refers to the visibility and accessibility of a variable within the code. Variables in JavaScript can have one of the following scopes: global or local.

Global variables:
Global variables are declared outside any function and are accessible throughout the program, both within functions and outside them. A global variable can be used by any part of the code. Example of a global variable:

```
var name = "Mary";

function greet() {
  console.log("Hello, " + name + "!");
}
```

```
greet(); // Output: "Hello, Mary!"
console.log(name); // Output: "Mary"
```

In this example, the variable name is declared outside the function greet() and is accessible both inside the function and outside it.

Global variables should be used with caution because they have a wide scope and can be modified from anywhere in the code. They can cause conflicts or undesirable effects if they are accidentally overwritten.

Local variables:
Local variables are declared within a function and are accessible only within that function. This means that local variables have a scope limited to the block of code in which they are declared. Example of a local variable:

```
function greet() {
  var name = "Bob";
  console.log("Hello, " + name + "!");
}

greet(); // Output: "Hello, Bob!"
console.log(name); // Output: ReferenceError: name is not defined
```

In this example, the variable name is a local variable defined within the function greet(). It can only be used within that function and is not accessible outside of it.

Local variables offer additional protection and modularity to the code, since they can only be used within the specific context in which they were declared. Each function has its own local scope, and variables defined in one function do not conflict with variables in other functions.

It is important to be careful when defining variables within blocks of code such as loops or if conditions. In JavaScript, there is no block scope, which means that a variable defined within a block of code will still be accessible outside that block.

In addition to global and local scope, JavaScript also has block scope introduced with the use of the **let** and **const** keywords since ECMAScript 6. These variables are limited to the scope of the block in which they are defined, such as an if block or a for loop. This provides greater precision and control over the scope of the variables.

Closure

In JavaScript, a closure is a function that has access to its context (environment) variables even after the function itself has been executed. This means that a closure stores a reference to variables that were present in the context in which it was created, allowing those variables to be accessed even when the function is called in a different context. Closures are a powerful and versatile concept that can be used to create functions with special behaviors and to manage the scope of variables more flexibly. Here is an example to better understand closures:

```
function createCounter() {
  var counter = 0;

  function increment() {
    counter++;
    console.log(counter);
  }

  return increment;
}

var myCounter = createCounter();

myCounter(); // Output: 1
myCounter(); // Output: 2
```

In this example, we have a createCounter() function that returns another increment() function. The createCounter() function contains a counter variable that is initialized to 0. The increment() function increments the counter value and prints it in the console.

When we call createCounter(), we get a closure, which is a copy of the increment() function with a reference to the context in which it was created. In this case, the closure retains the reference to the counter variable even after the createCounter() function has finished executing.

By assigning the closure returned by createCounter() to the myCounter variable, we can call myCounter() repeatedly to increment the counter and display the next value in the console.

Closures are useful in several situations, such as when we want to create functions that store state or when we want to maintain private variables within a module. Closures allow you to maintain data encapsulation, making it possible to access only context-relevant variables and functions.

It is important to understand that closures can also have memory management implications. When a closure keeps a reference to a variable alive, that variable cannot be deleted from memory as long as the closure exists. Therefore, care must be taken in how you use closures to avoid memory problems and memory leaks.

Array

Creating and manipulating arrays

Arrays are data structures that allow a collection of elements to be stored and manipulated. They can contain data of different types, such as numbers, strings, objects, and other arrays. Here is how to create and manipulate arrays in JavaScript:

Creating an array:
There are several syntaxes for creating an array in JavaScript. Here are some examples:

```
var numbers = [1, 2, 3, 4, 5]; // Creating an array of numbers

var fruit = ["apple", "banana", "orange"]; // Creating an array of strings

var mixed = [1, "two", true]; // Creating a mixed array

var empty = []; // Creation of an empty array
```

Accessing the array elements:
The elements of an array are indexed according to their position. The array index starts at 0 for the first element and continues sequentially. You can access the elements using the element access operator [].

```
var numbers = [1, 2, 3, 4, 5];

console.log(numbers[0]); // Output: 1
console.log(numbers[2]); // Output: 3
```

You can also **edit** a specific array element by assigning a new value to the corresponding index:

```
var numbers = [1, 2, 3, 4, 5];

numbers[2] = 10;
console.log(numbers); // Output: [1, 2, 10, 4, 5]
```

Array **length**:
The length property of an array returns the number of elements in the array.

```
var numbers = [1, 2, 3, 4, 5];

console.log(numbers.length); // Output: 5
```

Iteration on arrays

There are several options for iterating over the elements of an array. Some common methods for iterating over arrays will be listed below.

for:
You can use a traditional for loop to iterate over the elements of an array using the element index.

```
var numbers = [1, 2, 3, 4, 5];

for (var i = 0; i < numbers.length; i++) {
  console.log(numbers[i]);
}
```

forEach() method:
Arrays in JavaScript have a forEach() method that allows you to iterate over the elements without having to manually manage the index of the elements.

```
var numbers = [1, 2, 3, 4, 5];

numbers.forEach(function(number) {
  console.log(number);
});
```

The forEach() method requires a callback function that is executed for each element in the array. The current element is passed as an argument to the callback function.

for...of:
Starting with ECMAScript 6, you can use the for...of loop to iterate directly over the elements of an array without having to manage the index of the elements.

```
var numbers = [1, 2, 3, 4, 5];

for (var number of numbers) {
  console.log(number);
}
```

The for...of loop automatically iterates over each array element and assigns the current element to the specified variable (number in the example above).

map() method:
The map() method is used to iterate over the elements of an array and return a new array with the changes made to the elements.

```
var numbers = [1, 2, 3, 4, 5];
```

```
var doubled = numbers.map(function(number) {
  return number * 2;
});

console.log(doubled); // Output: [2, 4, 6, 8, 10]
```

The map() method requires a callback function that is called for each element in the array and returns a new value for that element. The end result is a new array with the modified elements.

Methods of arrays

In JavaScript, arrays have many built-in methods that allow you to manipulate and operate on array elements. Here are some of the most common methods for manipulating arrays:

push(): Adds one or more elements to the end of the array and returns the new length of the array.

```
var numbers = [1, 2, 3];
numbers.push(4, 5);
console.log(numbers); // Output: [1, 2, 3, 4, 5]
```

pop(): Removes the last element from the array and returns it.

```
var numbers = [1, 2, 3, 4, 5];
var lastElement = numbers.pop();
console.log(lastElement); // Output: 5
console.log(numbers); // Output: [1, 2, 3, 4]
```

shift(): Removes the first element from the array and returns it, reducing the length of the array.

```
var numbers = [1, 2, 3, 4, 5];
var firstElement = numbers.shift();
console.log(firstElement); // Output: 1
console.log(numbers); // Output: [2, 3, 4, 5]
```

unshift(): Adds one or more elements to the beginning of the array and returns the new length of the array.

```
var numbers = [2, 3, 4, 5];
numbers.unshift(1);
console.log(numbers); // Output: [1, 2, 3, 4, 5]
```

slice(): Returns a surface copy of a portion of the array selected by the start and end indexes. The original array is not modified.

```
var numbers = [1, 2, 3, 4, 5];
```

```
var portion = numbers.slice(1, 4);
console.log(portion); // Output: [2, 3, 4]
console.log(numbers); // Output: [1, 2, 3, 4, 5]
```

splice(): Modify the array by removing, replacing, or adding elements based on the specified indexes.

```
var numbers = [1, 2, 3, 4, 5];

// Removes two elements starting at index 2
numbers.splice(2, 2);
console.log(numbers); // Output: [1, 2, 5]

// Replaces one element at index 1
numbers.splice(1, 1, 'new element');
console.log(numbers); // Output: [1, 'new element', 5]

// Adds elements starting at index 2
numbers.splice(2, 0, 'element 1', 'element 2');
console.log(numbers); // Output: [1, 'new element', 'element 1', 'element 2', 5]
```

Arrays in JavaScript have many other useful methods, such as concat(), join(), reverse(), sort(), filter(), map(), reduce(), etc. Each of these methods has a specific purpose and offers an easy way to manipulate arrays according to your needs.

Multidimensional arrays

Multidimensional arrays are arrays that contain other arrays as elements. This makes it possible to create a data structure suitable for representing and manipulating complex data.

Creating a multidimensional array:
To create a multidimensional array, you can simply place an array inside another array. For example:

```
var arrayMulti = [[1, 2, 3], [4, 5, 6], [7, 8, 9]];
```

In this example, we created a multidimensional array with 3 internal arrays, each containing 3 numbers.

Accessing the elements of a multidimensional array:
To access the elements of a multidimensional array, you can use the element access operator [] in combination with array indexes. For example:

```
console.log(arrayMulti[0][1]); // Output: 2
console.log(arrayMulti[2][0]); // Output: 7
```

Editing the elements of a multidimensional array:
You can modify the elements of a multidimensional array by assigning a new value to the corresponding index. For example:

```
arrayMulti[1][2] = 10;
console.log(arrayMulti); // Output: [[1, 2, 3], [4, 5, 10], [7, 8, 9]]
```

In this case, we changed the value 6 in the array inside index 1, index 2.

Iteration on a multidimensional array:
You can use nested for loops to iterate over the elements of a multidimensional array. For example:

```
for (var i = 0; i < arrayMulti.length; i++) {
  for (var j = 0; j < arrayMulti[i].length; j++) {
    console.log(arrayMulti[i][j]);
  }
}
```

This code iterates through the internal arrays and prints each element.

Multidimensional arrays can be useful for representing structured data, such as an array of values, a game grid, or a table. Be sure to account for array indexes when accessing and editing elements in the multidimensional array.

Objects

Creating and manipulating objects

In JavaScript, objects are data structures that allow related values and functions to be grouped within a single entity. Objects consist of key-value pairs, where the key is a string that identifies the property and the value can be any type of data, such as numbers, strings, arrays, or even other objects.

Creating object:
You can create an object using the literal object syntax, which consists of curly brackets {}. You can assign properties and values to the object using the key: value format. For example:

```
var person = {
  name: "Bob",
  age: 30,
  profession: "Developer"
};
```

In this example, we created an object called "person" with three properties: "name," "age," and "profession," each with its own value.

Accessing the properties of an object:
You can access the properties of an object using the member access operator . followed by the name of the property. For example:

```
console.log(person.name); // Output: "Bob"
console.log(person.age); // Output: 30
console.log(person.profession); // Output: "Developer"
```

Editing the properties of an object:
You can change the value of an object property by assigning it a new value. For example:

```
console.log(person.age); // Output: 30
person.age = 35;
console.log(person.afe); // Output: 35
```

In this case, we changed the value of the property "age" from 30 to 35.

Adding new properties:
You can add new properties to an object by assigning them a value. For example:

```
person.city = "Rome";
console.log(person.city); // Output: "Rome"
```

In this case, we added a new property called "city" to the "person" object.

Deleting properties:

You can delete a property of an object using the delete operator. For example:

```
delete person.profession;
console.log(person.profession); // Output: undefined
```

In this case, we removed the "profession" property from the "person" object.

Objects in JavaScript can also contain **functions** as properties, which are called methods of the object. This allows you to define specific behaviors and actions for an object. To call an object method, you can use the syntax nameObject.nameMethod(). For example:

```
var person = {
  name: "Bob",
  greet: function() {
    console.log("Hello, I am " + this.name + "!");
  }
};

person.greet(); // Output: "Hi, I'm Bob!"
```

In this example, we created a method called "greet" that prints a greeting message using the name of the object.

Objects are a fundamental part of JavaScript and offer a powerful way to organize and manipulate data. You can access object properties, modify them, add new ones, and even delete properties you no longer need. Leveraging objects allows you to create complex data structures and model real-world concepts efficiently.

Properties and methods of objects

Properties are values associated with the object, while methods are functions that belong to the object itself.

Object **properties**:

Object properties are key-value pairs that describe the characteristics of the object. You can access properties using the syntax "nameObject.nameProperty" or "nameObject['nameProperty']". For example:

```
var person = {
  name: "Bob",
  age: 30,
  profession: "Developer"
};

console.log(person.name); // Output: "Bob"
console.log(person['age']); // Output: 30
```

In this example, "name," "age," and "profession" are the properties of the object "person."

Object **methods**:
Object methods are functions that belong to the object itself. They can be used to perform actions or process data about the object. You can define methods within an object like any other property. For example:

```
var person = {
  name: "Mario",
  greet: function() {
    console.log("Hello, I am " + this.name + "!");
  }
};

person.greet(); // Output: "Hi, I'm Mario!"
```

In this example, "greet" is a method of the "person" object. It is called using the syntax "nameObject.nameMethod()".

Access to properties

Dot notation:
Dot notation is the most common form of accessing object properties. You can use the member access operator . followed by the name of the property. For example:

```
var person = {
  name: "Bob",
  age: 30,
  profession: "Developer"
};

console.log(person.name); // Output: "Bob"
console.log(person.eta); // Output: 30
console.log(person.profession); // Output: "Developer"
```

In this example, we are accessing the "name," "age," and "profession" properties of the "person" object using dot notation.

Notation with square brackets:
You can also access object properties using square bracket notation []. This notation is especially useful when the property name contains special characters or when it is determined dynamically. For example:

```
var person = {
  name: "Bob",
  age: 30,
  profession: "Developer"
};
```

```
console.log(person['name']); // Output: "Bob"
console.log(person['age']); // Output: 30
console.log(person['profession']); // Output: "Developer"
```

In this example, we are using square bracket notation to access the properties of the "person" object.

Dynamic access to properties:
Square bracket notation is particularly useful when accessing properties dynamically. You can use variables or expressions to determine the name of the property to be accessed. For example:

```
var person = {
  name: "Bob",
  age: 30,
  profession: "Developer"
};

var prop = 'name';
console.log(person[prop]); // Output: "Bob"
```

In this case, we are using a prop variable to determine the name of the property to be accessed.

Verifying the existence of a property:
You can check whether an object has a particular property by using the in operator or the hasOwnProperty() method. For example:

```
var person = {
  name: "Bob",
  age: 30,
};

console.log('name' in person); // Output: true
console.log(person.hasOwnProperty('age')); // Output: true
console.log('profession' in person); // Output: false
console.log(person.hasOwnProperty('city')); // Output: false
```

In this example, we are using the in operator and the hasOwnProperty() method to check the existence of certain properties in the "person" object.

Iteration on objects

You can iterate over objects using several techniques. Below are some of the options available for iterating over objects.

"for...in" loop:
The "for...in" loop allows you to iterate over the properties of an object. This loop iterates over all enumerable properties of the object, including its methods. For example:

```
var person = {
  name: "Bob",
  age: 30,
  profession: "Developer"
};

for (var prop in person) {
  console.log(prop + ": " + person[prop]);
}
```

In this example, the "for...in" loop iterates over all properties of "person" and prints the property name and its value.

"Object.keys()" method:
The "Object.keys()" method returns an array containing the names of the enumerable properties of an object. You can use this array to iterate over properties. For example:

```
var person = {
  name: "Bob",
  age: 30,
  profession: "Developer"
};

var propArray = Object.keys(person);
for (var i = 0; i < propArray.length; i++) {
  var prop = propArray[i];
  console.log(prop + ": " + person[prop]);
}
```

In this example, "Object.keys(person)" returns an array containing ["name," "age," "profession"]. Next, we use a "for" loop to iterate over this array and access the properties of the "person" object.

"Object.entries()" method:
The "Object.entries()" method returns an array containing the key-value pairs of the enumerable properties of an object. You can use this array to iterate over properties. For example:

```
var person = {
  name: "Bob",
```

```
  age: 30,
  profession: "Developer"
};

var entries = Object.entries(person);
for (var i = 0; i < entries.length; i++) {
  var prop = entries[i][0];
  var value = entries[i][1];
  console.log(prop + ": " + value);
}
```

In this example, "Object.entries(person)" returns an array containing [["name", "Bob"], ["age", 30], ["profession", "Developer"]]. We use a "for" loop to iterate over this array and access the keys and property values.

It is important to note that the order of properties in JavaScript objects is not guaranteed and may vary between implementations. Therefore, when iterating over objects, the order of the properties cannot be relied upon.

DOM (Document Object Model)

Introduction to DOM

The Document Object Model (DOM) is a tree-like representation of the elements of an HTML or XML document that JavaScript can dynamically manipulate. It provides an interface for accessing, modifying, and manipulating elements, their attributes, and content within a Web page.

The DOM is fundamental to client-side JavaScript programming, as it allows you to interact with document elements and make changes in real time. Here is a brief introduction to the main features of the DOM:

- **Tree structure**: The DOM organizes HTML elements in a tree structure, where each element is a node. The root node is the document itself, and its descendants include the HTML elements, their attributes, and the text within them. You can access these nodes using methods and properties provided by the DOM.

- **Access to elements**: You can access HTML elements using DOM methods and properties, such as getElementById(), getElementsByClassName(), getElementsByTagName(), and querySelector(). These methods allow retrieving one or more elements based on specific selectors or criteria.

- **Element Manipulation**: You can manipulate DOM elements by modifying their attributes, contents, or styles. For example, you can change the text of an element, add or remove classes, change CSS styles, or add new elements dynamically.

- **Events**: The DOM allows you to handle events generated by user interaction, such as clicking a button or submitting a form. You can assign event handlers to specific elements using methods such as addEventListener() to perform specific actions when an event occurs.

- **DOM traversing**: You can traverse the DOM by moving between nodes and their parents, children, or siblings using properties such as parentNode, childNodes, nextSibling, and previousSibling. This allows you to navigate through the document structure and access related nodes.

The DOM is a powerful interface for interacting with elements on a Web page using JavaScript. Through DOM manipulation, you can create dynamic pages, update content in response to user actions, and change the appearance and behavior of elements on the page.

Selecting DOM elements

You can select Document Object Model (DOM) elements using several methods and selectors. Here is an overview of the main options available for selecting DOM elements:

getElementById():
This method returns the element with the specified ID. The ID must be unique within the document. For example:

```
var element = document.getElementById("myElement");
```

getElementsByClassName():

This method returns a collection of elements with the specified class. You can access the elements by using the index or by iterating over the collection. For example:

```
var elements = document.getElementsByClassName("myClass");
```

getElementsByTagName():

This method returns a collection of elements with the specified element name (e.g. "div", "p", "a", etc.). You can access the elements by using the index or by iterating over the collection. For example:

```
var elements = document.getElementsByTagName("div");
```

querySelector():

This method returns the first element that matches the specified selector. The selector can be a class, an ID, an element name, or a complex CSS selector. For example:

```
var element = document.querySelector("#myElement");
var element = document.querySelector(".myClass");
var element = document.querySelector("div");
var element = document.querySelector(".myClass span");
```

querySelectorAll():

This method returns a NodeList containing all the elements that match the specified selector. You can access the elements by using the index or by iterating over the NodeList. For example:

```
var elements = document.querySelectorAll(".myClass");
var elements = document.querySelectorAll("div");
var elements = document.querySelectorAll(".myClass span");
```

Manipulating the properties and contents of the elements

Manipulating the properties and contents of Document Object Model (DOM) elements allows dynamic changes to be made to the elements themselves.

Accessing element properties:

You can access the properties of DOM elements using dot notation. For example, to access the "innerText" property of an element to get or set its inner text, you can use the following code:

```
var element = document.getElementById("myElement");
var text = element.innerText; // gets the element's inner text
element.innerText = "New Text"; // sets the element's inner text
```

Manipulating the content of elements:
You can manipulate the content of elements using the "innerHTML" or "textContent" properties. The "innerHTML" property returns or sets the HTML within the element, also allowing you to insert dynamic HTML. The "textContent" property returns or sets plain text within the element, ignoring any HTML tags. For example:

```
var element = document.getElementById("myElement");
var html = element.innerHTML; // gets the element's inner HTML
element.innerHTML = "<p>New paragraph</p>"; // sets the element's inner HTML

var element2 = document.getElementById("myElement2");
var text = element2.textContent; // gets the element's internal text
element2.textContent = "New text"; // sets the element's internal text
```

Manipulation of element attributes:
You can manipulate element attributes using element properties or the "setAttribute()" method. For example, to get or set the value of an attribute as "src" of an image, you can use the following code:

```
var image = document.getElementById("myImage");
var src = image.src; // get the value of the src attribute
image.src = "new-image.jpg"; // sets the value of the src attribute
```

Adding and removing CSS classes:
You can add or remove CSS classes from elements using the "classList" property and its methods such as "add()" and "remove()." For example:

```
var element = document.getElementById("myElement");
element.classList.add("newClass"); // adds a class to the element
element.classList.remove("oldClass"); // removes a class from the element
```

Event Handling

Event handling in the DOM allows you to listen and respond to user actions, such as clicking a button, loading a page, or entering text into an input field. Here is how to handle events in the DOM using JavaScript:

Adding an event handler:
You can add an event handler to a DOM element using the "addEventListener()" method. This method requires two arguments: the type of event to listen for and the function to execute when the event occurs. For example, to add an event handler for a button click, you can use the following code:

```
var button = document.getElementById("myButton");
button.addEventListener("click", function() {
  // Actions to execute when button click occurs
});
```

Removing an event handler:

If you want to remove an event handler from an element, you can use the "removeEventListener()" method. This method requires the same arguments used for adding the event handler. For example, to remove an event handler for clicking a button, you can use the following code:

```
var button = document.getElementById("myButton");
var handler = function() {
  // Actions to execute when button click occurs
};

button.addEventListener("click", handler);

// Remove the event handler
button.removeEventListener("click", handler);
```

Event handling with separate functions:
A separate function can be defined as an event handler and assigned to an element. This allows you to separate the event logic from the main code. For example:

```
var button = document.getElementById("myButton");

function handlerClick() {
  // Actions to execute when button click occurs
}

button.addEventListener("click", handlerClick);
```

Event accessing:
Within an event handler, you can access the event object, which provides information about the event itself, such as the event type, target element, cursor coordinates, etc. You can use the event object as a parameter to your function. For example:

```
var button = document.getElementById("myButton");

function handlerClick(event) {
  // Actions to execute when button click occurs
  console.log("You clicked the button");
  console.log("Event type: " + event.type);
}

button.addEventListener("click", handlerClick);
```

Event handling in the DOM allows you to make web pages interactive and responsive to user input. You can listen for a wide range of events, such as clicking, loading, keystrokes, mouseover, and many others, and define actions to be performed in response to these events using JavaScript.

Error handling and debugging

Types of errors

Several types of errors can occur during code execution. Knowing these types of errors is important to better understand debugging and error handling in the language.

- **Syntax errors** occur when code does not follow the grammatical rules of the language. These errors can be caused by missing parentheses, misplaced commas, incorrect variable declarations, etc. When syntax errors occur, the code will not execute correctly and an error message will be displayed in the browser console or terminal.

- **Reference errors** occur when an attempt is made to access a variable or object that does not exist or is outside its scope. For example, if you try to access an undeclared variable or a DOM element that does not exist, a reference error will be generated.

- **Type errors** occur when invalid operations are performed on certain types of data. For example, if you attempt to perform division by zero, concatenate a string with a non-string value, or use a method not supported by a data type, a type error will be generated.

- **Logic errors** occur when code produces unexpected or incorrect results due to errors in programming logic. These errors can be more complex to detect and resolve because they are not caused by obvious syntax or type errors, but by poor design or incorrect instruction sequence.

- **Run-time errors** occur during code execution and can be caused by a variety of factors, such as nonexistent function calls, network or resource problems, asynchronous operations not handled properly, etc.

It is important to properly handle errors in your JavaScript code by using try-catch blocks or specific error handling statements. This way, you can catch errors and handle them appropriately, such as by displaying custom error messages or taking fallback actions to keep the application in a consistent state.

Using the try-catch block

The try-catch block is a construct in JavaScript used to handle errors in a controlled manner. It allows you to **try** a block of code where you suspect errors may occur and, if an error occurs, **catch** the generated exception and handle it appropriately. Here is how to use the try-catch block for error handling in JavaScript:

```
try {
  // Block of code where errors are suspected to occur.
  // Execute operations that might generate an exception
} catch (error) {
  // Block of code that is executed when an error occurs.
  // Handle the error appropriately
}
```

In the try block, enter the code you wish to try. If an error occurs during the execution of this block, control immediately switches to the corresponding catch block. The error is caught and passed as a parameter to the variable "error" in the catch block.

Here is a practical example:

```
try {
  var result = 10 / number; // attempt to perform a division
  console.log("Result:", result);
} catch (error) {
  console.log("An error occurred:", error);
}
```

In this example, we are trying to perform a division by a "number" variable that may not be defined or may be equal to zero. If an error occurs during division, the exception is caught in the catch block and an error message is displayed.

You can also use multiple catch blocks to handle different types of errors specifically. For example:

```
try {
  // Code block
} catch (error1) {
  // Handle error1
} catch (error2) {
  // Handle error2
} finally {
  // Code block always executed at the end, regardless of the error
}
```

The **finally** block is optional and contains code that is always executed at the end, regardless of whether or not an error occurs. It is useful for performing cleanup actions or resource releases.

The try-catch block is a powerful tool for handling errors in a controlled way in your JavaScript code. Use it to catch errors, provide feedback to the user, and keep the application flow in a consistent state even when exceptions occur.

Launching and handling custom exceptions

In JavaScript, you can throw and handle custom exceptions by using the throw construct to throw an exception and the try-catch block to handle it. This allows you to generate and handle specific errors in your code.

Throw a custom exception:
You can throw a custom exception using the throw construct. You can pass any value as an argument to throw, but commonly an error object is used to provide detailed information about the error. For example:

```
throw new Error("A custom error occurred");
```

You can customize the error message by passing a specific string as an argument to Error(). You can also extend the Error class to create custom errors with additional properties.

```
class MyError extends Error {
  constructor(message) {
    super(message);
    this.name = "MyError."
  }
}

throw new MyError("A custom error occurred");
```

Handling a custom exception:
To handle a custom exception, you can use the try-catch block. Within the try block, enter the code that might generate the exception. In the catch block, specify the type of error you want to handle and define the behavior to be performed when the error occurs. For example:

```
try {
  // Code block that could generate an exception
  throw new Error("A custom error occurred");
} catch (error) {
  // Code block to handle the exception
  console.log("Error:", error.message);
}
```

You can specify different catch blocks to handle specific types of errors. This allows you to handle different errors in different ways. For example:

```
try {
  // Block of code that could generate a custom exception
  throw new MyError("A custom error occurred");
} catch (error) {
  if (error instanceof MyError) {
    console.log("Custom error:", error.message);
  } else {
    console.log("Generic error:", error.message);
  }
}
```

Throwing and handling custom exceptions gives you more granular control over errors in your JavaScript code. You can create errors with specific information and handle them appropriately to provide better feedback to the user and keep the application in a consistent state.

Strumenti di debugging

There are several debugging tools available that can help you identify and fix errors in your code.

Browser Development Console:
The development console is a debugging tool built into most modern browsers. You can open the development console by pressing F12 on your keyboard and switching to the "Console" tab. Here you can view log messages, errors and warnings generated by your JavaScript code. You can also use methods such as console.log(), console.error(), console.warn() to send debug output to the console. For example:

```
console.log("Debug message");
console.error("Error!");
console.warn("Warning!");
```

Breakpoints:
You can set breakpoints in your JavaScript code using the browser's development console. Breakpoints allow you to suspend code execution at certain points and inspect the state of variables and data. You can place breakpoints directly in your code or in the "Sources" panel of the development console. For example:

```
// Set a breakpoint
debugger;

// More code to examine
```

Profiling tools:
Modern browsers also offer profiling tools that allow you to analyze the performance of your code. You can use these tools to identify parts of your code that take too long to run or cause unnecessary slowdowns.

Code printing:
An easy way to do debugging is to print values or messages in your JavaScript code using console.log() or alert(). This can be useful for checking the value of a variable or for displaying information during code execution. For example:

```
var name = "John";
console.log("The name is:", name);
```

Integrated development tools:
Some integrated development environments (IDEs) offer advanced debugging capabilities for JavaScript. For example, Visual Studio Code has built-in support for JavaScript debugging with the ability to set breakpoints, run step-by-step code, examine variables, and more.

These are just a few of the debugging tools available in JavaScript. Each development environment has its own specific features and tools. It is important to become familiar with the debugging tools available in your preferred development environment and use them to simplify the process of identifying and resolving errors in your code.

Asynchronous programming

Callbacks

Callbacks are an important feature of JavaScript that allows the asynchronous execution of code to be handled. A callback is a function that is passed as an argument to another function and is called following the completion of an asynchronous operation or event.

Callbacks are widely used to handle situations where an operation takes time to complete, such as retrieving data from a server or processing a file. Instead of blocking code execution while waiting for the operation to complete, a callback function is passed to the function that handles the asynchronous operation. When the operation is completed, the callback function is called with the results of the operation.

Here is a simple example of using callbacks:

```
function executeAsynchronousOperation(callback) {
  setTimeout(function() {
   var result = "Data retrieved from asynchronous callback";
   callback(result);
 }, 2000); // Simulates a delay of 2 seconds
}

function handleResult(result) {
  console.log("Result:", result);
}

executeAsynchronousOperation(handleResult);
```

In this example, the function executeAsynchronousOperation simulates an asynchronous operation that takes 2 seconds. The function runResult is passed as a callback. When the operation completes, the callback function is called with the result of the operation, which is then printed to the console.

Callbacks can also be used to handle events. For example, when a user clicks a button, a callback can be associated with the button's event handler function. The callback will be called when the click occurs.

Callbacks can be used to create more readable and maintainable asynchronous code. However, because of their nested nature, callbacks can lead to a phenomenon known as "callback hell," in which code becomes complex and difficult to read. To address this problem, other techniques such as Promises and Async/Await have been introduced.

Promises

Promises are a further evolution of callbacks in JavaScript and provide a more structured and manageable way to handle asynchronous operations and their return of results. Promises allow more readable and maintainable code to be written, avoiding the so-called "callback hell."

A Promise represents the asynchrony of an operation that can have two states: "pending" or "resolved." When a Promise is created, it is initially in a "pending" state. Once the asynchronous operation is successfully completed, the Promise switches to the "resolved" state, returning a value. In case of an error, the Promise transitions to the "rejected" state, returning an error reason.

Here is an example of the use of Promises:

```
function executeAsynchronousOperation() {
  return new Promise(function(resolve, reject) {
    setTimeout(function() {
      var result = "Data retrieved from asynchronous call";
      if (result) {
        resolve(result);
      } else {
        reject("Error during asynchronous operation");
      }
    }, 2000); // Simulates a delay of 2 seconds
  });
}

executeAsynchronousOperation()
  .then(function(result) {
    console.log("Result:", result);
  })
  .catch(function(error) {
    console.error("Error:", error);
  });
```

In this example, the executeAsynchronousOperation function returns a Promise. Within the Promise, an asynchronous operation (simulated via setTimeout) is executed. If the operation completes successfully, the resolve method is called passing the result. In case of an error, the reject method is called passing the reason for the error.

To handle the result of the Promise, the .then() method is used, which receives as an argument a function to execute when the Promise is resolved successfully. In case of an error, the .catch() method is used, which receives a function to execute when the Promise is rejected.

Promises also allow calls to be concatenated in a more readable way by using the .then() method multiple times. In this way, a series of asynchronous operations can be performed sequentially.

```
executeAsynchronousOperation()
  .then(function(result) {
```

```
    console.log("First result:", result);
    return executeOtherAsynchronousOperation();
  })
  .then(function(otherResult) {
    console.log("Other result:", otherResult);
  })
  .catch(function(error) {
    console.error("Error:", error);
  });
```

Promises offer a more structured approach to handling asynchronous operations, improving code readability and maintainability compared to nested callbacks. In addition, Promises can be combined with other features such as async/await to write even simpler and more intuitive asynchronous code.

Async/await

Async/await is another feature introduced in JavaScript to simplify and improve the handling of asynchronous operations. This syntax is based on Promises and provides a clearer and more readable way to write asynchronous code.

The async keyword is used to declare a function as asynchronous. Within a function declared as async, you can use the await keyword to pause code execution until a Promise is resolved. The operation followed by await can be any expression that returns a Promise.

Here is an example of using async/await:

```
function executeAsynchronousOperation() {
  return new Promise(function(resolve, reject) {
    setTimeout(function() {
      var result = "Data retrieved from asynchronous call";
      if (result) {
        resolve(result);
      } else {
        reject("Error during asynchronous operation");
      }
    }, 2000); // Simulates a delay of 2 seconds
  });
}

async function executeOperations() {
  try {
    var result = await executeAsynchronousOperation();
    console.log("Result:", result);
  } catch (error) {
    console.error("Error:", error);
  }
}
```

```
executeOperations();
```

In this example, the <u>executeAsynchronousOperation</u> function returns a Promise, as in the Promises example. The <u>executeOperations</u> function is declared as async to indicate that it contains asynchronous operations. Within <u>executeOperations</u>, the await statement is used to pause execution until the Promise is resolved or rejected.

The use of async/await simplifies the reading of asynchronous code, since it appears that the code is executed synchronously, avoiding the need for callbacks or concatenation of .then() methods. In addition, the use of try/catch allows for more elegant error handling.

It is important to note that functions declared as async always return a Promise, even if it is not explicitly declared with return. If an exception is thrown within an async function, the Promise will be rejected with the reason for the exception.

Error handling in the asynchronous domain

Error handling in the asynchronous scope in JavaScript can be addressed using Promises, the try-catch block, and callback functions. Let's look at how to handle errors in each of these situations.

Promises: When using Promises for asynchronous operations, you can use the .catch() method to catch errors. This method is called when a Promise is rejected ("rejected" status). Here is an example:

```
executeAsynchronousOperation()
 .then(function(result) {
   console.log("Result:", result);
 })
 .catch(function(error) {
   console.error("Error:", error);
 });
```

Try-catch block: If you use async/await, you can use the try-catch block to handle errors within asynchronous functions. The try block is used to enclose the asynchronous operation, while the catch block is used to handle errors. Here is an example:

```
async function executeOperations() {
 try {
  var result = await executeAsynchronousOperation();
  console.log("Result:", result);
 } catch (error) {
  console.error("Error:", error);
 }
}
```

Callback functions: If callback functions are used to handle asynchronous operations, errors can be handled within the callback functions themselves. Here is an example:

```
executeAsynchronousOperation(function(error, result) {
  if (error) {
    console.error("Error:", error);
  } else {
    console.log("Result:", result);
  }
});
```

In all these cases, it is important to handle errors appropriately to ensure a better user experience and prevent unexpected situations. You can log errors, display error messages to the user or perform corrective actions, depending on the needs of the application.

In addition, as explained in previous chapters, custom errors can be thrown using the throw keyword, creating objects of type Error. This allows you to define and handle custom exceptions in the asynchronous scope, improving code quality and maintainability.

JSON (JavaScript Object Notation)

Introduction to JSON

JSON (JavaScript Object Notation) is a lightweight and widely used data format for exchanging information between client and server. It is based on JavaScript object syntax, but can be used with many other programming languages.

JSON consists of a collection of key-value pairs, in which data are organized in a hierarchical structure. Keys are always strings, while values can be of different data types, including numbers, strings, Booleans, objects, arrays, and nulls.

Here is an example of a JSON object:

```
{
  "first_name": "Mario"
  "last_name": "Rossi",
  "age": 30,
  "address": {
    "street": "Via Roma",
    "city": "Milan"
  },
  "interests": [ "music", "sports", "travel" ]
}
```

In this example, we have a JSON object with several properties: first name, last name, age, address, and interests. The address object is itself a nested object, while interests is an array of strings.

JSON is widely used in the Web context for transferring data between client and server. For example, when making an HTTP request to a server for data, the server may respond by returning a JSON response containing the requested data.

Parsing and creating JSON objects

In JavaScript, you can use the JSON.parse() method to convert a JSON string to a JavaScript object and the JSON.stringify() method to convert a JavaScript object to a JSON string.

Parsing a JSON string into a JavaScript object:

```
var jsonString = '{"first_name": "Bob", "last_name": "Smith", "age": 30}';
var jsonObject = JSON.parse(jsonString);

console.log(jsonObject.first_name); // Output: Bob
console.log(jsonObject.last_name); // Output: Smith
console.log(jsonObject.age); // Output: 30
```

In this example, the JSON string "{"first_name": "Bob", "last_name": "Smith", "age": 30}" is converted to a JavaScript object using the JSON.parse() method. The properties of the JavaScript object can be accessed using dot notation.

Creating a JSON string from a JavaScript object:

```
var person = {
  first_name: "Bob"
  last_name: "Smith",
  age: 30
};

var jsonString = JSON.stringify(person);
console.log(jsonString); // Output: {"first_name": "Bob", "last_name": "Smith", "age":30}
```

In this example, the JavaScript person object is converted to a JSON string using the JSON.stringify() method. The resulting JSON string corresponds to the representation of the JavaScript object in JSON format.

You can optionally include a second parameter called "replacer" in the JSON.stringify() method. This parameter allows you to filter and manipulate the properties of the object during serialization. In addition, you can specify a third parameter called "spacing" to set the formatting of the JSON string with indentation and spacing.

```
var person = {
  first_name: "Mario"
  last_name: "Rossi",
  age: 30
};

var jsonString = JSON.stringify(person, ["first_name", "age"], 2);
console.log(jsonString);
/*
Output:
{
  "first_name": "Bob",
  "age": 30
}
*/
```

In this example, the JSON string will be generated including only the "name" and "age" properties of the person object and with a 2-character spacing for formatting.

Using the JSON.parse() and JSON.stringify() methods, you can easily convert between JavaScript objects and JSON strings, enabling the processing, transmission, and storage of structured data in the JSON format.

Data handling

Using the API

In JavaScript, APIs (Application Programming Interfaces) allow you to interact with external services, such as Web servers or RESTful services, to send and receive data.

It is important to note that the use of APIs can vary depending on the specifications of the API itself. Some APIs require authentication or sending additional parameters in the request. You should consult the documentation of the specific API to understand the specific details and approaches for API usage.

APIs offer a powerful ability to interact with external services to send and receive data. They are widely used in web development to integrate external functionality and exchange data with remote servers.

Fetch API e AJAX

In JavaScript, the Fetch API and AJAX (Asynchronous JavaScript and XML) are two common approaches for making asynchronous requests to a server and obtaining data or sending data to the server. Both methods allow communication with a server without having to completely reload the web page.

Fetch API:
The Fetch API is a modern API introduced in JavaScript that provides a simple and efficient way to make asynchronous HTTP requests. It uses the fetch() method to send requests and returns a Promise representing the response to the request. Here is an example of using the Fetch API to get JSON data from a server:

```
fetch('https://api.example.com/data')
 .then(response => response.json())
 .then(data => {
  console.log(data); // JSON data received
 })
 .catch(error => {
  console.error('An error occurred:', error);
 });
```

In this example, we use fetch() to send a GET request to the specified URL. Next, we use the .json() method on the response to extract the JSON data from the response. Finally, we use the .then() method to handle the Promise success case and the .catch() method to handle any errors.

AJAX (XMLHttpRequest):
AJAX is a more traditional approach to making asynchronous requests in JavaScript. It uses the XMLHttpRequest object to send HTTP requests to the server and receive data in response. Here is an example of using AJAX to get JSON data from a server:

```
var xhr = new XMLHttpRequest();
xhr.open('GET', 'https://api.example.com/data', true);
```

```
xhr.onreadystatechange = function() {
  if (xhr.readyState === 4 && xhr.status === 200) {
    var data = JSON.parse(xhr.responseText);
    console.log(data); // JSON data received
  }
};
xhr.send();
```

In this example, we create a new XMLHttpRequest object and configure it to make a GET request to the specified URL. We use the onreadystatechange property to define a callback function that is executed when the request state changes. In the callback, we check the status of the request (readyState) and the status of the response (status) to ensure that the request completes successfully. Next, we use JSON.parse() to convert the response into a JavaScript object.

Both methods, Fetch API and AJAX, allow us to make asynchronous requests and get data from the server. The Fetch API is more modern and offers a simpler syntax using Promise, while AJAX is a more traditional but still widely used approach. The choice between the two will depend on your needs and the support required by the browsers you intend to support.

Manipulating JSON data

Once you have received JSON data via an API in JavaScript, you can manipulate it and use it in your code to display or process it further.

Suppose you received a JSON response from an API using the Fetch API as shown above:

```
fetch('https://api.example.com/data')
  .then(response => response.json())
  .then(data => {
    // Handling of received JSON data
    console.log(data); // JSON data received
    // You can use the data here to display or process it further
  })
  .catch(error => {
    console.error('An error occurred:', error);
  });
```

Once you have obtained the JSON data, you can access their properties and use them in your code. For example, if the JSON data contains an array of objects representing users, you can iterate over them using a forEach loop:

```
fetch('https://api.example.com/data')
  .then(response => response.json())
  .then(data => {
    // Manipulation of the received JSON data
    data.forEach(user => {
```

```
      console.log(user.name); // Accessing the 'name' property of each user
  });
})
 .catch(error => {
  console.error('An error occurred:', error);
 });
```

You can use the same techniques to access the properties of JSON objects and modify them to suit your needs. For example, you can filter data, sort objects by certain properties, perform calculations, or display data in an HTML page using DOM manipulations.

Remember that the JSON data received may vary depending on the API and its structure. Be sure to understand the structure of the received JSON data and adapt your manipulation code accordingly.

ES6 and advanced syntax

Introduction

ES6, short for ECMAScript 6, is the sixth edition of the ECMAScript standard, which defines the JavaScript language. It was published in 2015 and introduced a number of new features and improvements to the JavaScript language.

ES6 is a major update that brought several new features to the language, making writing JavaScript code more efficient, concise, and powerful.

Below we will explore on some of the major features introduced in ES6.

Arrow functions

Arrow functions in JavaScript are a more concise syntax for declaring functions. They were introduced in ECMAScript 6 (ES6) and offer several advantages over traditional function syntax.

Here is an example of how to declare an arrow function:

```
const square = (x) => {
  return x * x;
};
```

In this example, the square function is declared using the arrow function syntax. The variable square is assigned to the arrow function that takes a parameter x. The body of the function is defined in curly brackets {} and the result of multiplying x * x is returned.

The syntax of arrow functions offers several advantages:

- **More concise syntax**: Arrow functions are shorter than traditional functions, which makes them more readable and less verbose.

- **Context Binding**: Arrow functions maintain the context binding of their external scope. This means that the value of this within an arrow function is determined by the context in which it was defined, and is not affected by how it is called.

- **No binding of the arguments object**: Arrow functions do not have their own copy of the arguments object. Therefore, if you need to access the arguments passed to the function, you should use the rest parameters syntax (...args) or default arguments.

Here are some additional examples of arrow functions with even more concise syntax:

```
// Arrow function with only one parameter
const double = x => x * 2;
```

```
// Arrow function with no parameter
const sayHello = () => console.log("Hello!");

// Arrow function with implicit body and implicit returned value
const sum = (a, b) => a + b;
```

In the first example, the arrow function "double" takes only one parameter x and returns its double. Since there is only one parameter, the parentheses around x can be omitted.

In the second example, the arrow function "sayHello" has no parameters and simply prints a hello message on the console. Again, the parentheses can be omitted since there are no parameters.

In the third example, the arrow function "sum" takes two parameters a and b and returns their sum. Since the body of the function is a single expression, the curly brackets and return keyword can be omitted.

Template literals

Template literals are a feature that allows you to create more readable and flexible strings in JavaScript. They are delimited by backticks (`) instead of the traditional single or double quotation marks.

With template literals, you can create multiline strings without the need to concatenate several lines of text. Just insert the desired lines inside the backticks, and the string will retain its original formatting.

Here is an example of how to use template literals:

```
const name = 'Mary';
const message = `Hello ${name}!
Welcome to our website.
We hope you have a good experience here.`;

console.log(message);
```

In this example, we use template literals to create a message variable that contains a multiline string. Within the string, we use the ${name} syntax to insert the value of the name variable within the text. This is called "string interpolation" and allows variable values to be dynamically inserted within strings without the need for explicit concatenation.

Another interesting feature of template literals is the ability to execute JavaScript expressions within the curly brackets within the template. This can be useful for performing complex operations or calculations during string creation.

```
const a = 10;
const b = 5;
const result = `The sum of ${a} and ${b} is ${a + b}.`;
```

```
console.log(result);
```

Instead, in this example we perform an addition operation within the template string to calculate the sum of two numbers. The output will be "The sum of 10 and 5 is 15."

In summary, template literals are a very useful feature in JavaScript that simplify the creation of complex, multiline strings with dynamic values. They allow you to improve code readability and avoid tedious concatenation of strings.

Destructuring assignment

Destructuring assignment is a feature that allows you to extract values from arrays or objects and assign them to separate variables more concisely. This syntax makes it easier and more readable to access values within arrays and objects.

For example, let's look at how to use destructuring assignment with an array:

```
const myArray = [1, 2, 3];
const [a, b, c] = myArray;

console.log(a); // Output: 1
console.log(b); // Output: 2
console.log(c); // Output: 3
```

In this example, we declared an array myArray containing three elements. Using destructuring assignment, we extracted the values of the array and assigned them to variables a, b and c. Each variable corresponds to the corresponding element in the array.

The destructuring assignment can also be used with objects:

```
const myObject = { name: 'Mary', age: 25 };
const { name, age } = myObject;

console.log(name); // Output: Mary
console.log(age); // Output: 25
```

In this example, we have an object myObject with two properties: name and age. Using destructuring assignment, we extracted the properties and assigned them to variables with the same name. We can then access the values of the properties through the corresponding variables.

The destructuring assignment can also be used to assign default values in case a property or element is not present in the array or object:

```
const myArray = [1, 2];
const [a, b, c = 3] = myArray;
```

```
console.log(a); // Output: 1
console.log(b); // Output: 2
console.log(c); // Output: 3
```

In this case, we assigned a default value of 3 to the variable c. Since the array myArray does not have a third element, the variable c assumes the default value.

Classes and inheritance

In JavaScript, classes and inheritance allow objects to be created and the relationships between them to be managed in a more structured, object-oriented way.

In simple terms, a class is a model or structure that defines the characteristics and behavior of an object. A class can contain properties (variables) and methods (functions) that describe the state and actions of the object that will be created based on that class.

Inheritance is a concept that allows new classes to be created based on existing classes by inheriting their properties and methods. The existing class is called the "parent class" or "superclass," while the newly created class is called the "child class" or "subclass." The child class inherits all the properties and methods of the parent class and can add or overwrite existing ones to suit its specific needs.

Inheritance allows classes to be organized in a hierarchical structure, in which child classes inherit common behavior and features from the parent class, allowing code reuse and the creation of more specialized class hierarchies.

To define a class in JavaScript, we can use the keyword **class** followed by the class name. Within the class, we can define methods and properties that describe the behavior and state of the objects created by that class. For example:

```
class Person {
  constructor(first_name, last_name) {
    this.first_name = first_name;
    this.last_name = last_name;
  }

  greet() {
    console.log(`Hello, I'm ${this.first_name} ${this.last_name}`);
  }
}
```

In this example, we defined a Person class with a constructor that accepts the first and last name as parameters and assigns them to the object's first and last name properties. We also defined a greet() method that prints a greeting message using the object's properties.

To create an instance of a class, we can use the keyword **new** followed by the class name, passing any arguments required by the constructor. For example:

```
const person1 = new Person('Mary', 'Smith');
person1.greet(); // Output: Hello, I'mMary Smith
```

In the example above, we created an instance of the Person class called person1 by passing the values 'Mary' and 'Red' to the constructor. We then called the greet() method on the instance, which prints the corresponding greeting message.

To implement inheritance between classes in JavaScript, we can use the **extends** keyword to indicate that one class inherits from another class. For example:

```
class Student extends Person {
  constructor(first_name, last_name, course) {
    super(first_name, last_name);
    this.course = course;
  }

  study() {
    console.log(`${this.first_name} ${this.last_name} is studying ${this.course}`);
  }
}
```

In this example, we have defined a Student class that inherits from the Person class. We use the constructor of the parent class (super()) to call the constructor of the Person class and assign first and last name values. We also add a new course property specific to the student. Finally, we defined a study() method that prints a message about the student's study.

We can then create instances of the Student class and use both the methods inherited from the Person class and those specific to the Student class:

```
const student1 = new Student('Bob', 'Greens', 'Math');
student1.greet(); // Output: Hi, I'm Bob Greens
student1.study(); // Output: Bob Greens is studying Math
```

In conclusion, classes and inheritance in JavaScript allow us to create more organized structures and model relationships between objects. We can define classes with methods and properties, create instances of these classes, and use the methods and properties to manage the behavior of objects.

Modules

Introduction to modules

Modules in JavaScript are a mechanism for organizing code into isolated, reusable units. Below are some key advantages and features of modules:

- **Code organization**: Modules allow code to be divided into separate files, each of which contains a specific part of the application. This makes it easier to manage and understand the code, especially for complex projects.

- **Encapsulation**: Modules allow you to define separate scopes for variables and functions. This means that variables and functions defined within a module are not globally accessible unless explicitly exported. This promotes encapsulation and reduction of unwanted dependencies between different parts of the code.

- **Reusability**: Modules allow the creation of components or libraries that can be easily imported and used in different parts of the project. This promotes code reuse, reducing duplication and simplifying maintenance.

- **Declarative dependencies**: Modules allow dependencies between different components of the project to be explicitly declared. This makes it easier to understand which modules depend on others and promotes more efficient dependency management.

- **Local scoping**: Modules create their own local scoping, which means that variables and functions defined within a module are accessible only within that module, unless explicitly exported. This avoids name collisions and conflicts between global variables.

- **Dynamic loading**: Modules allow dynamic loading of code, which means that modules can be loaded and unloaded at runtime as needed. This can improve application performance, since unneeded modules do not have to be loaded until they are actually used.

- **Native support**: As of ECMAScript 6 (ES6), modules are natively supported in JavaScript. This means that you can use import and export syntax without having to depend on external libraries or additional compilation tools.

In conclusion, using modules in JavaScript offers many benefits, including better code organization, encapsulation of variables and functions, code reusability, and more efficient dependency management. Modules are a key element in developing modular and scalable applications in JavaScript.

Import ed export

Import and export of modules are managed through the import and export keywords. These keywords allow us to define which elements (variables, functions, classes) of a module are to be made available to other modules and which elements are to be imported from other modules.

To export elements from a module, we use the **export** keyword followed by the declaration or definition of the elements we wish to export. Let's look at some examples:

```
// Export a constant
export const name = 'Mary';

// Export a function
export function hello() {
  console.log(`Hello, ${name}`);
}

// Export a class
export class Person {
  constructor(name) {
    this.name = name;
  }

  greet() {
    console.log(`Hello, I am ${this.name}`);
  }
}
```

In this example, we are exporting a name constant, a greet() function, and a Person class from the current module.

To import elements from one module into another module, we use the **import** keyword followed by the name of the element we wish to import, in curly brackets {}. Here is an example:

```
// Import a constant
import { name } from './module.js';

console.log(name); // Output: Mary

// Importing a function
import { greet } from './module.js';

greet(); // Output: Hello, Mary

// Importing a class
import { Person } from './module.js';

const person = new Person('Bob');
person.greet(); // Output: Hi, I am Bob
```

In this case, we are importing the name constant, the greet() function, and the Person class from the "module.js" module. Note that the .js extension is used to indicate that this is a JavaScript file.

You can also use the default import to import a default element from a module. In this case, you do not need to use curly brackets. For example:

```
// module.js
export default function greet() {
  console.log('Hello!');
}

// main.js
import greet from './module.js';

greet(); // Output: Hello!
```

In this case, we are exporting the greet() function as the default export from the "module.js" module and importing it as a variable called greet in the "main.js" file.

Dependency management

In managing dependencies in JavaScript modules, there are several techniques that can be used to ensure that modules are properly imported and that dependencies are resolved properly. Here are some of the main techniques for managing dependencies in JavaScript modules:

- **Import and export**: Use the import and export keywords to import and export modules. In this way, you can explicitly specify dependencies between modules.

- **Package manager**: Use a package manager such as npm (Node Package Manager) or Yarn to manage external project dependencies. Package managers allow you to declare dependencies in the package.json file and easily install them with the npm install or yarn install command.

- **Module system**: Use a module system such as CommonJS or ECMAScript (ES) Modules to organize and manage JavaScript modules. CommonJS is primarily used for server-side environments such as Node.js, while ES Modules is the native module system supported by modern browsers.

- **Bundler**: Use a bundling tool such as Webpack, Rollup or Parcel to combine modules and their dependencies into a single production-optimized JavaScript file. Bundlers allow you to manage dependencies efficiently, reducing the number of network requests and improving application performance.

- **Dependency injection**: Use dependency injection to pass dependencies from one module to another via parameters or properties. This approach promotes greater code flexibility and testability, allowing dependencies to be easily replaced with custom implementations during testing or initialization.

- **Asynchronous modules**: If you are working with asynchronous modules, such as when using dynamic module loading or handling asynchronous requests, you must carefully manage dependencies so that modules are available when requested.

Advanced event handling

Bubbling e capturing

In JavaScript, event bubbling and event capturing are two phases of event propagation within the Document Object Model (DOM).

Event bubbling occurs when an event is triggered on a child element and propagates upward through the parent element hierarchy. In other words, the event is handled by the child element, then propagated to the parent elements. This process continues until it reaches the root element of the document (usually the HTML document). During the bubbling phase, you can capture the event on the different parent elements and handle it.

Here is an example to better understand event bubbling:

```
// HTML
<div id="parent">
 <div id="child">
  <button id="button">Click me!</button>
 </div>
</div>

// JavaScript
document.getElementById('button').addEventListener('click', function() {
 console.log('You clicked the button!');
});

document.getElementById('child').addEventListener('click', function() {
 console.log('You clicked the child element!');
});

document.getElementById('parent').addEventListener('click', function() {
 console.log('You clicked the parent element!');
});
```

In the example above, when the button is clicked, the following outputs will be displayed in the console:

```
You clicked the button!
You clicked the child element!
You clicked the parent element!
```

The click event is triggered first on the button, then on the child element and finally on the parent element, propagating along the chain of parent elements.

On the other hand, event capturing is the stage prior to bubbling. During the capturing phase, the event is handled by the parent elements before reaching the target element. This behavior can be enabled by using the third true parameter in the addEventListener method:

```
document.getElementById('parent').addEventListener('click', function() {
  console.log('You clicked the parent element!');
}, true);

document.getElementById('child').addEventListener('click', function() {
  console.log('You clicked the child element!');
}, true);

document.getElementById('button').addEventListener('click', function() {
  console.log('You clicked the button!');
}, true);
```

In this case, when the button is clicked, the following outputs will be displayed in the console:

```
You clicked the parent element!
You clicked the child element!
You clicked the button!
```

The event is handled first by the parent element, then by the child element, and finally by the target button.

In summary, event bubbling and event capturing are two phases of event propagation in the DOM. Event bubbling involves propagation from the child element to the parent element, while event capturing involves propagation from the parent element to the child element. Both mechanisms can be used to handle events in a flexible and controlled manner within the element hierarchy.

Delegation of events

Event delegation is a technique in JavaScript that allows events to be handled on a parent element instead of on specific child elements. This approach is useful when you have many similar child elements on which you want to apply the same type of event handling.

Event delegation takes advantage of event propagation (bubbling) in the DOM. Instead of assigning an event handler to each child element, you assign an event handler to the parent element. When an event occurs on a child element, the event is propagated upward in the parent element hierarchy until it reaches the parent element with the assigned event handler. Then, you can determine the specific child element on which the event occurred and take the necessary actions.

Here is an example of delegating events to handle clicks on a list of <li> elements:

```
// HTML
<ul id="myList">
  <li>Element 1</li>
  <li>Element 2</li>
  <li>Element 3</li>
</ul>
```

```
// JavaScript
document.getElementById('myList').addEventListener('click', function(event) {
  if (event.target.tagName === 'LI') {
    // The event was triggered on a <li> element.
    console.log('You clicked on: ' + event.target.textContent);
  }
});
```

In this example, an event handler is assigned to the parent <ul> element. When one of its child elements <li> is clicked, the event is propagated upward to the <ul> element and the event handler is executed. Within the event handler, we check whether the event was triggered on a <li> element by checking the tagName property of the event.target object. If the event was triggered on a <li> element, a message is displayed in the console.

Event delegation offers several advantages:

- **Efficiency**: With a single event handler on the parent element, you avoid having to assign and manage events on each child element individually, improving code efficiency.

- **Dynamic handling**: Event delegation works even with child elements dynamically added or removed from the DOM. Even if the child elements change, the event handler assigned to the parent element remains valid.

- **Code reduction**: Since only one event handler is needed, the code is cleaner and more readable, without the need to duplicate the same code to handle similar events on different child elements.

Event delegation is a powerful technique for handling events in JavaScript, allowing you to simplify your code and improve efficiency. However, it is important to take care to correctly specify the desired target element within the event handler to avoid unwanted behavior.

Touch and swipe events

Touch and swipe events are specific to touch inputs on mobile devices and are used to manage user interactions such as touching, swiping, and dragging on elements.

Touch events occur when a user touches the device screen with a finger. Common touch events include "touchstart" (start of touch), "touchmove" (finger movement during touch) and "touchend" (end of touch). Event handlers can be assigned to these events to respond to user actions. For example:

```
elemento.addEventListener('touchstart', function(event) {
  // Logic to be executed when starting touch
});

elemento.addEventListener('touchmove', function(event) {
  // Logic to be executed during touch motion
});
```

```
elemento.addEventListener('touchend', function(event) {
  // Logic to be executed at the end of touch
});
```

Swipe events, on the other hand, occur when a user swipes his or her finger rapidly across the screen in a certain direction. Swipe events can be handled by combining touchstart, touchmove and touchend events. For example, to detect a swipe to the right, the following code can be used:

```
var startX, startY;

elemento.addEventListener('touchstart', function(event) {
  startX = event.touches[0].clientX;
  startY = event.touches[0].clientY;
});

elemento.addEventListener('touchend', function(event) {
  var endX = event.changedTouches[0].clientX;
  var endY = event.changedTouches[0].clientY;

  var deltaX = endX - startX;
  var deltaY = endY - startY;

  if (Math.abs(deltaX) > Math.abs(deltaY) && deltaX > 0) {
    // Swipe to the right
    // Logic to be executed for swiping to the right
  }
});
```

In the example above, you track the start coordinates of the touch in the "touchstart" event handler. In the "touchend" event handler, you calculate the end coordinates of the touch and determine whether the horizontal displacement (deltaX) is greater than the vertical displacement (deltaY). If it is and the horizontal displacement is positive, logic for swiping to the right is executed.

Customized events

In JavaScript, custom events can be created to extend the functionality of predefined events and allow communication between different code components. Custom events are useful when you want to notify other parts of the application of a particular event or pass specific data along with the event.

To create a custom event, you can use the Event class in the modern browser. Here is an example of how to create and trigger a custom event:

```
// Creation of the custom event
var customEvent = new Event('customEvent');

// Adding data to the custom event
```

```
customEvent.data = { message: 'This is a custom event!' };

// Dispatch the custom event on a specific element
var element = document.getElementById('myElement');
element.dispatchEvent(customEvent);
```

In the example above, a new custom event called "customEvent" is created using the Event class. Next, additional data is added to the custom event using a custom property called "date". Finally, the custom event is triggered on the element with the ID "myElement" using the dispatchEvent() method.

To listen for and handle a custom event, an event handler must be added to the affected element using the addEventListener() method. For example:

```
var element = document.getElementById('myElement');
element.addEventListener('customEvent', function(event) {
  console.log('Custom event unleashed!');
  console.log(Data: ', event.data);
});
```

In the example above, an event handler is added for the custom event "customEvent" on the element with the ID "myElement". When the custom event is triggered, the event handler is executed and displays a message in the console along with the event data.

Using custom events, a custom communication system can be created within the application, allowing different parts of the code to communicate with each other in a flexible and structured way.

Mouse and keyboard

You can manage mouse and keyboard events to interact with users.

Mouse events:

"**click**": Occurs when an element is clicked with the mouse button.
"**mouseover**": Occurs when the mouse cursor enters the area of an element.
"**mouseout**": Occurs when the mouse cursor exits the area of an element.
"**mousedown**": Occurs when the mouse button is pressed on an element.
"**mouseup**": Occurs when the mouse button is released on an element.
"**mousemove**": Occurs when the mouse cursor is moved within an element.

Keyboard events:

"**keydown**": Occurs when a keyboard is pressed and held down.
"**keyup**": Occurs when a keyboard is released after being pressed.
"**keypress**": Occurs when a keyboard is pressed and released.
"**input**": Occurs when the value of an input field is changed.

Here is an example of how to handle mouse and keyboard events in JavaScript:

```
// Handling the click event
var button = document.getElementById('myButton');
button.addEventListener('click', function(event) {
  console.log('You clicked the button!');
});

// Handling the keydown event
document.addEventListener('keydown', function(event) {
  console.log('You clicked the button: ' + event.key);
});

// Handling the input event
var input = document.getElementById('myInput');
input.addEventListener('input', function(event) {
  console.log('The value of the input has been changed: ' + input.value);
});
```

In the example above, an event handler for the "click" event is added to the button with the ID "myButton". When the button is clicked, a message is displayed in the console.

An event handler for the "keydown" event is also added to the document. When a key is pressed on the keyboard, a message is displayed in the console with the pressed key.

Finally, an event handler for the "input" event is added to the input element with the ID "myInput." When the input value is changed, a message is displayed in the console with the new input value.

Browser API

Introduction to browser APIs

Browser APIs are a set of features and methods made available by modern browsers to enable web developers to interact with the browser itself and its execution environment. These APIs provide a wide range of features that enable developers to create dynamic and interactive web applications.

They are implemented within the browser itself and are accessible through JavaScript. They provide developers with access to features such as the DOM (Document Object Model) to manipulate HTML elements, event handling, HTTP requests, geolocation, local storage, and much more.

Browser APIs are supported by all major modern browsers, such as Chrome, Firefox, Safari and Edge, and conform to the standards set by the World Wide Web Consortium (W3C).

The window object

In JavaScript, the window object represents the browser window in which the code is executed. It is a global object that provides access to several features and properties related to the browser window.

Here are some of the main features provided by the window object:

- **DOM manipulation**: The window object contains methods and properties to access and manipulate the DOM of the current web page. For example, you can use window.document to get the document object, which represents the current HTML document, and use its methods and properties to manipulate DOM elements.

- **Event handling**: You can use the window object to handle browser window events, such as loading the page (window.onload), resizing (window.onresize), closing the window (window.onbeforeunload), and many others.

- **Timers**: The window object provides setTimeout() and setInterval() methods to create timers that execute certain functions after a certain period of time or at regular intervals.

- **Managing windows and frames**: You can use the window object to open new windows or frames in the browser using the window.open() method. You can also access other open windows in the browser using the window.opener method.

- **Location and history management**: The window object provides methods and properties to manage the location of the browser window, such as window.location to get or set the current URL, window.history to manage the browsing history, and window.navigator to get information about the user's browser.

- **Interaction with the browser**: The window object provides methods to interact with the browser, such as window.alert() to show an alert window, window.prompt() to prompt the user to enter a value, and window.confirm() to prompt the user for confirmation.

- **Cookie handling**: You can use the window object to read and write cookies using the document.cookie method. Cookies are small pieces of data stored on the user's computer and can be used to maintain state or store session information.

Managing Cookies

Cookie management in JavaScript allows you to read, write, and manipulate cookies that are stored in the user's browser. Cookies are small text files that are sent from the web server to the browser and are stored on the user's computer. Cookies are commonly used to store session information, user preferences, and other browsing-related data.

To manage cookies in JavaScript, you can use the following properties and methods of the document object:

document.cookie: This property allows you to get or set the value of cookies. When you read document.cookie, it returns a string containing all cookies separated by semicolons. You can also assign a value to document.cookie to set a new cookie or overwrite an existing cookie. For example:

```
// Reading cookies
console.log(document.cookie);

// Setting a new cookie
document.cookie = "name=John Doe; expires=Fri, 31 Dec 2023 23:59:59 GMT; path=/";
```

expires: This attribute allows you to set the expiration date of the cookie. You can specify a date in GMT format to indicate when the cookie will expire. When the expiration date is reached, the cookie is automatically deleted from the browser. For example:

```
document.cookie = "name=John Doe; expires=Fri, 31 Dec 2023 23:59:59 GMT; path=/";
```

path: This attribute specifies the path to the URL with which the cookie is associated. If you set a path, the cookie will be available only for those pages that are in that path. For example:

```
document.cookie = "name=John Doe; path=/myapp";
```

domain: This attribute specifies the domain of the URL with which the cookie is associated. If you set a domain, the cookie will only be available for that domain and its subdomains. For example:

```
document.cookie = "name=John Doe; domain=example.com";
```

secure: This attribute specifies whether the cookie can only be sent over secure HTTPS connections. If you set secure to true, the cookie will only be sent over HTTPS connections. For example:

```
document.cookie = "name=John Doe; secure";
```

To read a specific cookie, you can create a function that parses the string returned by document.cookie and returns the desired cookie value. For example:

```
function getCookie(param) {
  const cookies = document.cookie.split("; ");
  for (let i = 0; i < cookies.length; i++) {
    const cookie = cookies[i].split("=");
    if (cookie[0] === param) {
      return cookie[1];
    }
  }
  return null;
}

console.log(getCookie("name")); // Returns the value of the "name" cookie
```

Remember that cookies are subject to security restrictions, such as same-origin policy and maximum cookie size. Be sure to use cookies in accordance with privacy regulations and consider using more secure alternatives such as access tokens or server-side sessions when necessary.

Controlling navigation

In the context of JavaScript, history and location objects provide functionality to control navigation and interact with the current browser URL. Let us now see how to use them.

The **history object** provides methods and properties to manage the browser's browsing history.

- history.back(): Returns to the previous page in the history.
- history.forward(): Go to the next page in the history.
- history.go(n): Go forward or backward n pages in the history.
- history.length: Returns the number of pages in the browser history.

Example:

```
// Back to the previous page
history.back();

// Go to the next page
history.forward();

// Go back 2 pages
history.go(-2);

// Returns the number of pages in the history
console.log(history.length);
```

The **location object** provides information about the current URL in the browser and allows you to interact with it.

- location.href: Returns the full URL of the current page.
- location.reload(): Reloads the current page.
- location.assign(url): Navigates to the specified URL.
- location.replace(url): Navigates to the specified URL, replacing the current URL in the history.
- location.search: Returns the query string of the current URL.
- location.pathname: Returns the path to the current URL.

Example:

```
// Returns the full URL of the current page
console.log(location.href);

// Reloads the current page
location.reload();

// Navigates to a new URL
location.assign('https://www.example.com');

// Navigates to a new URL, replacing the current URL in the history
location.replace('https://www.example.com');

// Returns the query string of the current URL
console.log(location.search);

// Returns the pathname of the current URL
console.log(location.pathname);
```

Using the history and location objects, you can check browser browsing history, navigate to new URLs, reload the current page, and get information about the current URL. This allows you to customize navigation and react to user actions within your web application.

Local data storage

Local data storage can be managed using the localStorage API. localStorage is an object that allows data to be stored persistently in the user's browser.

Here is how to use **localStorage** to store and retrieve data:

Data storage:
You can store data in localStorage using the setItem(key, value) method. key is a string representing the name of the data to be stored, while value is the actual value you want to store.

```
// Stores a value in the localStorage
localStorage.setItem('name', 'John');
```

Data stored in localStorage are stored as strings. So, if you want to store a JavaScript object, you must convert it to a string using the JSON.stringify() method.

```
const person = { name: 'John', age: 30 };

// Stores the person object as a string in the localStorage
localStorage.setItem('person', JSON.stringify(person));
```

Data retrieval:
You can retrieve data stored in the localStorage using the getItem(key) method. Pass the key of the data you want to retrieve and you will get the corresponding value.

```
// Retrieves the value stored in the localStorage
const name = localStorage.getItem('name');
console.log(name); // Output: John

// Retrieves the stored object as a string and converts to a JavaScript object
const storedPerson = JSON.parse(localStorage.getItem('person'));
console.log(storedPerson); // Output: { name: 'John', age: 30 }
```

Data removal:
You can remove a specific data item from the localStorage using the removeItem(key) method.

```
// Removes the data stored with the key 'name'
localStorage.removeItem('name');
```

You can also clear all data stored in the localStorage using the clear() method.

```
// Clear all data stored in the localStorage
localStorage.clear();
```

It is important to note that the data stored in the localStorage is domain-specific and can only be accessed in the same domain origin. In addition, data stored in the localStorage is persistent and remains available even after the browser is closed and reopened.

Local data storage using localStorage is useful for storing information such as user preferences, application status, or other data that must be maintained even after the page is closed. However, it is important to use localStorage carefully and make sure not to store sensitive or excessively large data, since the data is accessible client-side.

Geolocation

Geolocation in JavaScript allows the user's geographic location to be obtained using the browser or mobile device. This functionality can be used to provide personalized experiences, location-based services, or for other geolocation-related purposes.

Verifying Support:
Before using geolocation, check whether the user's browser or mobile device supports this feature. You can do this by checking if the navigator.geolocation object is defined.

```
if (navigator.geolocation) {
  // Geolocation is supported
} else {
  // Geolocation is not supported
}
```

Getting the current position:
To get the user's current position, use the getCurrentPosition() method of the navigator.geolocation object. Pass a callback function that will be executed with the Position object containing the position data.

```
navigator.geolocation.getCurrentPosition(function (position) {
  const latitude = position.coords.latitude;
  const longitude = position.coords.longitude;

  console.log('Latitude:', latitude);
  console.log('Longitude:', longitude);
});
```

The position is returned as a Position object that contains geographic coordinates, such as latitude and longitude, within the position coords object.

Error handling:
During position retrieval, errors may occur. It is important to handle these errors correctly to provide appropriate feedback to the user.

```
navigator.geolocation.getCurrentPosition(
  function (position) {
    // Success: getting the current position
  },
  function (error) {
    // Error: handle geolocation error
    console.log('Geolocation error:', error.message);
  }
);
```

The most common errors are PERMISSION_DENIED (user denied permission to geolocate) and POSITION_UNAVAILABLE (current location cannot be obtained).

Geolocation in JavaScript can be used for a wide range of applications, such as interactive maps, location-based services, user tracking, and more. However, it is important to respect the user's privacy and seek appropriate consent before accessing their location.

Browser notifications

Browser notifications in JavaScript allow alerts or messages to be sent to the user directly from the browser, even when the application or website is not actively in the foreground. Browser notifications can be used to provide updates, notifications of important events, or to engage the user even when they are not actively interacting with the application.

Verifying Support:
Before using browser notifications, check whether the user's browser supports this feature. You can do this by checking if the Notification object is defined.

```
if (window.Notification) {
  // Browser notifications are supported
} else {
  // Browser notifications are not supported
}
```

Requesting permission:
Before sending notifications, you must request permission from the user. You can do this using the requestPermission() method of the Notification object. This method will return a promise representing the permission status.

```
Notification.requestPermission().then(function (permission) {
  if (permission === 'granted') {
    // Permission has been granted
  } else if (permission === 'denied') {
    // Permission has been denied
  }
});
```

It is important to note that the permission request can only be executed as a result of a user action, such as a button click.

Creating and displaying notifications:
After obtaining permission, you can create and display notifications using the Notification object. You can set the title, body, and other options to customize the notification.

```
if (Notification.permission === 'granted') {
  const options = {
    body: 'This is the body of the notification',
    icon: 'path/to/icon.png',
```

```
};

  const notification = new Notification('Title of the notification', options);
}
```

Once the notification is created, it will be displayed to the user's device operating system. The appearance and behavior of notifications may vary depending on the browser and operating system used.
Browser notifications offer an effective way to engage and inform users even when they are not actively engaged in the application. However, it is important to use notifications carefully and respect the user's privacy. Always seek appropriate consent before sending notifications and use them responsibly to provide relevant and useful information.

Time management

Time management in JavaScript allows you to perform operations at specific times or create delays between actions. This can be useful for scheduling the execution of certain functions, creating animations, periodically updating data, or handling other time-based operations.

Delays:
The **setTimeout()** function allows you to delay the execution of a function after a certain period of time expressed in milliseconds. You can use it to create delays between actions or to execute an operation once after a certain time interval.

```
setTimeout(function() {
  // Code to execute after the delay
}, 2000); // Delay of 2000 milliseconds (2 seconds)
```

Periodic execution:
The **setInterval()** function allows you to execute a function periodically at specified time intervals. You can use it to create animations, update data in real time, or perform other repeated operations.

```
setInterval(function() {
  // Code to execute at each interval
}, 1000); // Interval of 1000 milliseconds (1 second).
```

You can stop the periodic execution by using the clearInterval() function and passing the ID returned by setInterval().

Immediate execution:
The **requestAnimationFrame()** function allows you to execute a function at the beginning of the next browser rendering cycle. It is particularly useful for creating smooth and optimized animations, since it synchronizes with the refresh rate of the screen.

```
function animation() {
  // Code for animation
```

```
  requestAnimationFrame(animation);
}

// Start the animation
requestAnimationFrame(animation);
```

Time management:
The **Date()** object allows you to get the current date and time or create instances of specific dates. You can use it to handle time-based events, calculate differences between dates, and other time-related operations.

```
const now = new Date(); // Current date and time

const specificDate = new Date('2023-01-01'); // Instance of a specific date

const timestamp = Date.now(); // Unix timestamp of the current instant in milliseconds
```

Time management in JavaScript offers many ways to control the execution of your operations based on delays, intervals, or timed events. However, it is important to pay attention to the efficiency and proper use of time management functions, avoiding excessive delays or overly intense update cycles that could slow down your application or consume resources unnecessarily.

Offline storage

Browser cache in JavaScript is a temporary storage mechanism for storing resources (such as HTML files, CSS, JavaScript, images, etc.) on the user's device for faster access and better user experience. By using browser cache, you can make web pages available offline and reduce the network load required to obtain resources.

To use the browser cache, you can take advantage of the Cache API provided by the browser. The Cache API allows you to create a custom cache in which you can store and retrieve resources.

Creating a cache:

```
// Opens a cache with a specific name
caches.open('cache_name').then(function(cache) {
  // Performs operations on the cache
});
```

Adding resources to the cache:

```
// Gets the specified cache
caches.open('cache_name').then(function(cache) {
  // Adds a resource to the cache
  cache.add('url_resource');
});
```

Retrieval of resources from cache:

```
// Gets the specified cache
caches.open('cache_name').then(function(cache) {
  // Retrieves a resource from the cache
  cache.match('url_resource').then(function(response) {
    // Performs operations with the resource
  });
});
```

Removal of resources from cache:

```
// Gets the specified cache
caches.open('cache_name').then(function(cache) {
  // Removes a resource from the cache
  cache.delete('url_resource');
});
```

Using the browser cache offers several benefits, including faster page loading speed, the ability to view pages offline, and reduced network traffic. However, it is important to manage the cache properly, updating obsolete resources and handling any errors when retrieving resources from the cache.

Optimization and performance

Best practices for improving performance

"Best practices" are a set of recommended guidelines and principles for developing high-quality software. Here are some best practices for improving JavaScript performance:

- **Minimize the number of expensive operations**: Avoid computationally intensive or repeated operations within loops or callbacks. Try to optimize complex algorithms and use more efficient algorithms whenever possible.

- **Use asynchronous programming**: Take advantage of asynchronous features such as Promises and async/await to handle time-consuming operations, such as API calls. This avoids blocking the main thread and improves the responsiveness of the application.

- **Limits the use of globals**: Minimizes the use of global variables since they can cause conflicts and make debugging more difficult. Limit their use only when strictly necessary.

- **Avoid duplication of code**: Identify repetitive portions of code and reuse them using functions or modules. This reduces the amount of duplicate code and simplifies maintenance.

- **Optimize DOM manipulation**: Minimize DOM access and manipulation. Store references to frequently used DOM elements and use efficient methods such as querySelector and querySelectorAll.

- **Use caching**: Leverages browser caching or local storage to store frequently used data. This reduces network dependency and improves application performance.

- **Reduce the number of network requests**: Combine and minimize CSS and JavaScript files to reduce the number of requests to the server. Use gzip compression to reduce the size of transferred files.

- **Performs resource prefetching**: Uses prefetching to download necessary resources, such as images or CSS files, in advance to reduce the loading delay.

- **Use lazy loading**: Load resources only when they are needed, such as images on a page. This reduces the initial load and speeds up the loading time.

- **Monitor performance**: Use tools such as the Chrome Developer Tools to analyze application performance. Identify the parts of the code that take the longest and make appropriate optimizations.

Asynchronous loading of resources

Asynchronous resource loading in JavaScript allows external files or resources, such as scripts, style sheets, or data, to be loaded independently of the rest of the page. This technique helps improve the overall performance of the application by allowing the browser to continue performing other tasks while resources are downloaded in the background.

Async/Defer attributes: The async and defer attributes can be used in the <script> element to control the asynchronous loading of scripts. The **async** attribute indicates that the script can be loaded and executed asynchronously, without blocking page rendering. The **defer** attribute indicates that the script should be executed only after the document has been parsed, maintaining the relative order of the scripts.

```
<script src="script.js" async></script>
<script src="script.js" defer></script>
```

Dynamic script loading: You can dynamically create <script> elements using JavaScript and assign them the URL of the file to be loaded. This allows you to control the exact timing of script loading and execution.

```
const script = document.createElement('script');
script.src = 'script.js';
document.body.appendChild(script);
```

XMLHttpRequest (XHR): The XHR object allows you to make asynchronous HTTP requests to download data or resources from a server. You can use XHR to upload text files, JSON, XML or binary resources such as images.

```
const xhr = new XMLHttpRequest();
xhr.open('GET', 'data.json', true);
xhr.onreadystatechange = function() {
  if (xhr.readyState === 4 && xhr.status === 200) {
    const data = JSON.parse(xhr.responseText);
    // Manage the downloaded data
  }
};
xhr.send();
```

Fetch API: The Fetch API provides a modern interface for making asynchronous HTTP requests. You can use it to fetch resources such as text files, JSON, images, and more.

```
fetch('data.json')
  .then(response => response.json())
  .then(data => {
  // Manage the downloaded data
})
  .catch(error => {
  // Handle the loading error
```

```
});
```

These are just a few examples of how you can implement asynchronous resource loading in JavaScript. The best approach depends on the type of resource being loaded and the specific needs of the application. Using asynchronous loading helps improve the user experience by reducing loading times and allowing the browser to continue performing other tasks in parallel.

Resource prefetching

Resource prefetching in JavaScript is a technique that allows resources such as images, stylesheets, or scripts that may be required later to be downloaded in advance. This process is performed in the background by the browser to reduce loading times and improve the user experience.

Prefetching the <link> tag: You can use the rel="prefetch" attribute in the <link> tag to specify the resources you want to download in advance. For example, if you know that a CSS file or image will be needed later, you can include a <link> tag for prefetching in your HTML document.

```
<link rel="prefetch" href="styles.css">
<link rel="prefetch" href="image.jpg">
```

Prefetching the <a> tag: If you have links on your Web site that point to external pages or resources, you can use the rel="prefetch" attribute in the <a> tag to tell the browser to prefetch those resources.

```
<a href="page.html" rel="prefetch">Link to the page</a>
```

Prefetching via JavaScript: You can also use JavaScript to prefetch specific resources. For example, you can dynamically create a <link> element or use the Image object to download an image in the background.

```
// Prefetching a CSS file
const link = document.createElement('link');
link.rel = 'prefetch';
link.href = 'styles.css';
document.head.appendChild(link);

// Prefetching an image
const image = new Image();
image.src = 'image.jpg';
```

Automatic prefetching: Some browsers also support automatic prefetching, in which they autonomously prefetch resources deemed relevant to the page. This is done based on the analysis of users' browsing data.

It is important to note that resource prefetching should be used with caution, as it can increase network load and server resources. Be sure to identify critical resources for initial rendering and focus on prefetching those and avoid offloading unnecessary or large resources.

Also, keep in mind that resource prefetching may vary from browser to browser and may not be supported by all versions. Therefore, you should test the performance and effectiveness of prefetching on your specific execution environment.

Lazy loading

Lazy loading is a technique used in the Web context to improve page loading performance. It consists of initially loading only the essential content of the page, deferring the loading of other elements such as images, scripts or components that are not immediately visible to the user.

The goal of lazy loading is to reduce the initial page load time, allowing the user to quickly view the main content and improving the overall browsing experience. As the user scrolls down the page or interacts with it in some way, additional resources needed are dynamically loaded.

Initially, replace the "src" attribute of images with a "data-src" attribute that contains the URL of the image to be loaded.

```
<img data-src="path/to/image.jpg" alt="Image description">
```

Uses JavaScript to detect when the image becomes visible in the area displayed by the user, such as when the scroll reaches the position of the image.

```
window.addEventListener('scroll', function() {
  const images = document.querySelectorAll('img[data-src]');

  for (let i = 0; i < images.length; i++) {
    const img = images[i];
    const rect = img.getBoundingClientRect();

    // If the image is visible in the area displayed by the user
    if (rect.top < window.innerHeight) {
      // Replace the "data-src" attribute with "src" to load the image
      img.src = img.dataset.src;
      img.removeAttribute('data-src');
    }
  }
});
```

This implementation loads images only when they become visible to the user, avoiding loading all images at once during the initial page load.

Lazy loading can be used not only for images, but also for other elements such as scripts, components, or dynamic content. The main goal is to reduce the initial loading time, thus improving the user experience.

Outro

Dear Reader,

You have walked through the pages of this book like an explorer into a fascinating world, a world of code, creativity, and unlimited potential. You have learned about JavaScript, the language that powers the Web and has opened the door to a universe of opportunities.

You overcame early obstacles, discovering the secrets of variables and data types, learning to dance with control structures and orchestrate your functions in harmony. You understood that parentheses and semicolons are like notes in a score, which together make up melodies that come to life in your browser.

You had the courage to dive into the sea of objects, swimming between properties and methods, bringing out creative and solid solutions. You have faced cycles, loops of experience that guided you in creating and modifying arrays, across dimensions that only your imagination could conceive.

You have walked through the DOM, that mysterious realm that connects your code to your visible world, manipulating elements and bringing them to life through events and interactions. You have experienced the power of APIs, where you have found treasures like geolocation and notifications, enriching your applications with incredible functionality.

But it's not just about code. It's about your desire to discover, to learn and to grow. It's about making your mark on the vast universe of the Web, about creating experiences that enchant and engage, that push the limits of your imagination.

Always remember that you are the director of your story, the composer of your code. Don't let any obstacle stop you, because you have learned to overcome challenges, find creative solutions, and persist until you reach your goals.

Your journey in the world of JavaScript does not end here. There are always new horizons to explore, new topics to discover, new techniques to master. Keep your passion ignited, meet challenges with enthusiasm, and remember that improvement is a continuous journey.

Thank you for choosing this book as your guide on your journey into the world of programming. I hope it has ignited a spark within you that will drive you to explore, create, and share your talents with the world.

Happy journey, dear reader. May your code always be elegant, may your ideas shine like diamonds in the source code. The world is ready to welcome your creations. Step forward and make your mark on the vast universe of the Web.

Best wishes and good luck with your code!